Relax

IN A MINUTE ▶▶

Tony Wrighton is an NLP (Neuro-Linguistic Programming) Trainer and Master Practitioner. His self-development audiobooks have sold over 100,000 copies and have been Top 10 bestsellers on iTunes in many countries around the world. In addition to his work as an NLP coach, Tony is a TV and radio presenter.

www.tonywrighton.com

Relax
IN A MINUTE ▶▶

10 STEPS TO INSTANT CALM

Tony Wrighton

2 4 6 8 10 9 7 5 3 1

Published in 2011 by Virgin Books, an imprint of Ebury Publishing
A Random House Group Company

Copyright © Tony Wrighton 2011

Tony Wrighton has asserted his right under the Copyright, Designs and
Patents Act 1988 to be identified as the author of this work.

The Random House Group Limited Reg. No. 954009

Addresses for companies within the Random House Group can be found at:
www.randomhouse.co.uk

A CIP catalogue record for this book is available from the British Library.

The Random House Group Limited supports The Forest Stewardship
Council [FSC], the leading international forest certification organisation.
All our titles that are printed on Greenpeace-approved FSC-certified
paper carry the FSC logo. Our paper procurement policy can be found at:
www.rbooks.co.uk/environment.

Mixed Sources
Product group from well-managed
forests and other controlled sources
www.fsc.org Cert no. TT-COC-002139
© 1996 Forest Stewardship Council
FSC

Printed in the UK by CPI Bookmarque, Croydon, CR0 4TD

ISBN 9780753522554

To buy books by your favourite authors and register for offers, visit
www.rbooks.co.uk

Contents ▶▶

Contents

Introduction ▸▸

Every relaxation technique in this book takes a minute or less. If you don't believe me, flip to a random page right now and have a go at something. Go on. In just one minute, you will start to feel more relaxed.

Too often in the past self-help has been sharp-suited men ordering you across hot coals, or blokes with ponytails waving incense around, telling you, 'change doesn't come quickly'. That was all a bit too much like hard work. No thanks. This is different. It's down-to-earth and on your level. It works quickly and efficiently, which I've found is particularly important with people who are desperate to relax.

So why *did* you start reading this? Perhaps it was because of stress or a lack of calm caused by something in your life? This could be in any area, such as work, relationships, money, arguments, anxiety, internal thoughts, time (or lack of . . .), age, family, divorce, loss of loved ones, deadlines, illness, sex issues, weight gain, anger, loneliness or low self-esteem.

It might also be because you are nervous in some way, perhaps you have a big speech or presentation coming up, you're starting a new job or even going to a party where you don't know very many people.

Whatever your reason for wanting to learn to relax, this book will work for you. The exercises have been specifically designed so that you can fit them to suit your individual circumstances. It's not much fun dwelling on all the reasons why we might feel stressed, fearful and unable to unwind. From now on, you'll find the chapters deal with positive ways to help you relax, whatever your situation.

You'll read about: the famous sportsman who got out a pen and drew on his clothing to help him relax at critical moments; the author and businessman who is so laid back he only checks his email once a week; and even how acting like a rock star can help you in your quest for relaxation.

You'll also learn how to use email, Facebook, Twitter, iPhones and modern technology to help you to relax. And how switching off helps you to relax too.

Some people say, 'How can this stuff possibly make a difference when I've been worrying about it for years, and you say it only takes a minute to get better?'

In fact, if that's the case and you have been worrying about something for a long time, these techniques are absolutely the best thing you could possibly do. Many people live with stress and worry for ages without ever doing anything about it. I've made it easy to take the first step. And the second . . . the third . . . and the fourth . . . And from there who knows what you can achieve.

If you feel you are clinically depressed, or so stressed that you simply can't cope, then please see a doctor. If you have physical symptoms such as headaches, feeling ill, nausea or high blood pressure then, again, see a doctor. If you are epileptic please consult your doctor before using the techniques in this book. They are not meant to replace medical advice. However this book can help you make huge changes and start to relax.

Some people, especially those who don't get enough sleep, sometimes want to drop off when they use the stuff I talk about. For that reason, do not practise any of these techniques while driving. Only use them when it is safe to do so. And if you are somebody who is sleep-deprived, then you'll probably be turning to Chapter 4, Sleep.

One final thought. Keep going. Don't give up. If you meet a challenge, don't worry – that's normal – honest. Nobody has it all their own way. It's how you deal with that challenge. For more on the value of persistence and effort and how to keep at it, go to Chapters 9, The Postcard Plan and 10, The Future. The more effort you put in, the more reward you will get and the more relaxed a person you'll become.

CHAPTER ONE

Instant
Relaxation ▶▶

As Donna hauled herself out of bed, she realised that yet again she hadn't had eight hours' sleep. From the moment the alarm went off it was go, go, go, day after day. She already felt tired, and the day hadn't even begun. The kids had to be dressed, breakfast made, and then she had to dress herself and negotiate the commute to work.

Once there, she had to deal with her stressful boss. Or 'No-need', as they called him. ('No-need to get so upset!') Who wouldn't get stressed when No-need was so ridiculously demanding, picking on people for no good reason? Even the energy it took to stay out of his way stressed her out.

In the past she could go home and quietly unwind from all that. She used to enjoy getting home and idly thumbing

through a magazine for half an hour, or even having a little sleep on the sofa, and she'd found that a really good way to de-stress. Of course, she couldn't do that these days. When she got home there were kids to feed, nappies to wash and bottoms to be wiped! These days, she didn't feel so good at coping with it all. There was so much stress in the day, and she didn't feel able to unwind and relax.

Donna needed something that would work instantly. To instantly change the way she felt. Because she didn't have more than a minute to spare . . .

You have picked up this book because you find it hard to de-stress and relax. Like Donna, you want something that is going to work *now*.

So, before we go any further, here are three of my very best relaxation techniques that you can use instantly: The Spot; The Float; Bounce! This chapter is solely designed to enable you to relax quickly in situations that stress you out.

▶▶ *The Spot* starts working instantly. It is effective because at some point in your past you have felt relaxed, so we're going to use that memory to help you start to feel more relaxed now.

▶▶ *The Float*: Are you stressed, uptight or nervous? Do you fancy the idea of feeling the light, relaxing sensation of 'floating' around the room? The Float is adapted from an ancient relaxation ritual.

▶▶ *Bounce!* Are you feeling bouncy? This is another instant technique to use before a stressful situation. Notice how you start to change the way you *see* yourself.

The Spot

There was a famous sportsman who won the biggest tournament in his sport. Throughout the four days of competition he had drawn a small red spot on his clothing. Eventually the TV cameras picked up on it and, after he'd won, journalists asked him about this strange red spot.

It turned out he'd been working with a brilliant sport psychologist called Karl Morris to help his concentration levels. Dr Morris had worked out that by placing a coloured spot somewhere where he could see it often, he could get the sportsman to remind himself of what he was supposed to do at certain key moments. Every time he looked at the spot, it made him feel a certain way.

So, are you ready to give it a go?

Linking thoughts and emotions to colours is something I've been using for years and I have found it hugely effective. It works by making use of the amazing way that the brain links a visual stimulus to a thought. You must follow the specific instructions below though, or it doesn't work.

First, pick the colour you'd like to use.

Your options are:

▶▶ *Blue*: The colour of the ocean and the sky, and generally associated with calm and peacefulness.

▶▶ *Green*: The colour of nature, and calming and easy on the eye. Hospitals often paint walls light green because it relaxes patients.

I've tried a number of other colours over the years, but generally blue and green seem to work the best. Other colours have different associations. Yellow, for example, can be associated with a 'speeding of the metabolism' – not really ideal when you're trying to achieve a state of relaxation. And red isn't ideal either. It is the most emotionally intense colour, and one associated with – among other things – danger.

You might ask why the sports-psychologist worked with a red spot, rather than a blue one. Well, Dr Morris asked the sportsman what the colour was that he associated with focusing and keeping his concentration. He said 'red'. Simple as that. As we're going for relaxation, not focus, I would recommend blue and green as a great starting point, but by all means try different colours if you want.

These coloured spots become even more powerful when used alongside sophisticated memory association techniques to help you feel calm. Here is what you need to do.

1   *Get some coloured spot stickers in your chosen colour. (If you don't have any coloured stickers handy, just find a scrap of paper in your chosen colour until you can get some proper stickers.)*

2   *Stick one somewhere you'll see it often, but not constantly (see the Hint box on p. 10 for details).*

3   *Once you've placed your coloured spot, think of a specific time when you felt deeply relaxed. It might be lying by the pool on holiday, slouching in a comfy chair watching TV – any time when you felt relaxed. Think of that time now as you look at the spot.*

Associate as closely as you can with the memory, hearing what you heard at the time and making the sounds clear and crisp, seeing exactly what you saw and making the colours vivid as you continue to look at your spot and remember how relaxed you felt. (1 minute)

4 Now notice how you feel more relaxed whenever you happen to look at the spot.

Want to add some extra emotions onto your spot? Come up with some other ways that you'd like to feel (such as calm, controlled or happy). Follow the same memory process, watching your spot for a full minute each time.

5 Only leave the spot there for 24 hours. After this, either change the colour, or remove it and put a new coloured spot somewhere else.

This works effectively as long as you absolutely load up the spot with your desired emotion. I've been using a coloured spot on my phone. I just glanced down at it while writing this, and had an unexpectedly vivid flashback to my recent relaxing holiday in Thailand.

But I've found the usefulness of the spot starts to diminish over time. That's why the best time to use it is over a 24-hour period. After that, it's better to change the colour or the position of the spot, and load the feelings on again.

HINT

- Great places to put the spot: your mobile phone (front or back), computer screen, wallet, a bathroom mirror, the fridge, your keys or key-ring, the cover of this book. In other words, choose anything that you look at quite often during the day.

The Float

What makes this different from many other relaxation techniques is that you do it while you're walking. The principles behind 'walking meditation' have been around in various forms for thousands of years, and they're more relevant than ever because of the crazy number of distractions that we face in modern life.

So why did I call this 'The Float'? Well, this technique combines the principles of walking meditation with deep breathing and a special rhythm that calms the mind and body down. I find the result is a strange feeling of slowly floating as I walk. See if you agree:

1 *Start breathing slowly in for four counts and then slowly out for four counts. Count in your mind as you breathe. 'IN, 2, 3, 4, OUT, 2, 3, 4'. (1 minute)*

2 *Now lightly tap your thumb on each finger of your hand, starting on your index finger and working outwards to your little finger. Get a repetition going as you say, 'IN, 2, 3, 4', going from your index finger and tapping outwards, and then*

as you say, 'OUT, 2, 3, 4', again tapping from your index finger outwards. (1 minute)

3 *Now combine the breathing, the counting and the tapping. (1 minute)*

4 *For the final minute, slowly walk around the room while breathing, counting and tapping. For an even more effective rhythm, make sure each step coincides with the numbers and the thumb taps. You'll find this slows down the tapping, which is good. (1 minute)*

OK – here's a question. Are you finding it quite hard to combine everything at once? Good. It should take your full attention for the minute. If you find you have time to think about your shopping list *as well as* breathing, counting, tapping and walking, you may not be doing it properly.

If you find you're breathing too quickly, slow your steps down so you can slow your breathing down. This I find one of the most effective parts of The Float. It forces me to walk slower. With such a focused yet clear mind, it feels like floating.

This is adapted from an ancient yoga routine called Kirtan Kriya. It suggests that you should chant 'Sa, Ta, Na, Ma', instead of counting. These are believed to be primal sounds that can provide us with emotional balance. Kirtan Kriya requires a longer time period to practise, and the instructions must be followed exactly, so I'll leave you to do your own research if you would like to do a longer, more exact routine.

One more thing. Interruptions are okay on your walk. I decided to do The Float on the way to the shops today, and within ten seconds of leaving the house I bumped into a friend. You'll be pleased to know that I didn't just stand there in front of her, gazing vacantly and silently tapping my fingers. That might have looked a bit weird.

If you bump into somebody you know or are interrupted, put your minute-long meditation on hold. That's fine. Just accept it, and be sure to go for the full minute when you start again.

I find this a powerful way to relax and change the way I feel. Sometimes I find it so relaxing that I want to lie down and have a nap afterwards. When I do it outside I am also amazed at how much more aware I am of my surroundings than usual. I normally end up walking really slowly and calmly. It has that effect.

Start to use The Float daily as part of your relax routine. Once you get used to this, you can start to incorporate 'floating' into your everyday life. Float to the shops. Float to the train station. Float wherever you like.

Bounce!

Lucy had a terror of public speaking. This was an immediate problem as she was at a conference in Kuala Lumpur and that afternoon she was speaking to over 50 delegates. As she sat there, she thought about how she always blushed when she was nervous, and how even at school her teacher used to tell her to 'stand up straight in front of the class' and 'speak up'. ('Thanks, Mr Morgan.')

Bounce! is good for managing how you react to stressful thoughts and situations. Are you stressed? Do you want to relax right now? Let's Bounce! you into a different state:

1 *You need to work out what different, positive, bouncy state you would like to Bounce! yourself into. How would you like to feel? Make an image of how that would look in your mind. Make it big and bright, and put yourself in the picture, so that you very clearly see how positive things look when you feel this way.*

2 *Briefly make an image in your mind of how you look when you're stressed-out or anxious. For some people, this can be distressing, so make the picture black and white and quite grainy so it is hard to see. Make any sounds muffled and quiet.*

3 *Put your different, bouncy state right in the corner of this stressed-out image. Make it the size of a tiny little bouncy ball in the corner of the image.*

4 *When you're ready, Bounce! your positive state so that it grows really big, comes much closer and completely covers the old, unwanted picture. As you do it, say, 'Bounce!'*

   The unwanted picture melts away into the background. Now look at your huge bouncy state in front of you. Bright colours, clear, great sounds, and good feelings.

5 *Now clear your mind. Think about something entirely different, such as what you will have for dinner tonight. This bit is important.*

6 *Go through steps 1) to 5) again. Bounce! at least five or six times again over the course of a full minute with exactly the same process, until you have problems seeing the unwanted image, and you can't feel those unpleasant thoughts any more. Bounce! more quickly each time you go. (1 minute)*

By the way, exclaiming 'Bounce!' in a crowded coffee shop is a fairly guaranteed way to get attention. So if you're somewhere busy, you can do the Bounce! bit silently.

When Lucy bounced, what she was chuffed about was how it instantly stopped her from blushing so much. She said, 'I just find that I'm thinking less about blushing. That makes me feel less anxious, and so I blush less, and think more about how I'd like to appear and feel.'

That's it. One of the effective things about Bounce! is that it works differently for everybody. It is your own individual technique. You simply pick how you'd like to feel, and Bounce! into it.

However busy you are, you can hopefully always find at least one minute to squeeze in a moment of relaxation. Working mum Donna could. At moments of extreme irritation with No-need, she would 'go for a cup of tea'. She would take one minute out and do The Float while she was walking to the canteen. Occasionally she would put a small green spot inside her purse, and at random times during the day she would catch a glimpse of it. And she started using Bounce! when she woke up. Donna said that she enjoyed feeling 'a bit more bouncy' throughout the day.

TO-DO LIST – REMINDERS

▶▶ *The Spot*: An amazing visual relaxation tool. Get some blue/green spot stickers. Load up this spot sticker with intense feelings of relaxation. Then put it somewhere you'll see it often. (1 minute)

▶▶ *The Float*: Combine counting, walking, breathing and tapping your fingers to distract your mind fully. When you do it right, you'll experience a strange floating sensation. (1 minute)

▶▶ *Bounce!*: Manage how you react to stressful thoughts and situations. Make a big picture in your mind of how relaxed you'd like to look and feel. Then make a brief image of how you feel now. Have the new, 'bouncy' image as a little ball bouncing in the corner, and then Bounce! it right on top of the old image. Repeat until you can't see the old image any more. (1 minute)

CHAPTER TWO

Quiet

Julie saw an attractive guy. 'Wow!' she thought. She wanted to ask him out for coffee. And then her internal voice started up, 'What if he says no?' And then, 'He won't like you anyway.' She ended up doing nothing. Same old story . . .

She was asked to give a fifteen-minute presentation to some colleagues. She said, 'Yes', and then 'inner Julie' started up again. 'What if you forget what you were supposed to say? You might make a fool of yourself.'

And when she looked in the mirror, her internal voice didn't see the attractive, fun woman she was. Her internal voice told her, 'You are a bit fat round the hips. And look at those wrinkles.'

Yes, Julie was irritatingly good at talking herself down. She was understandably keen to quieten down all that inner chatter, but was sceptical that it could be done.

Inner silence can have an amazing effect on how we think and act, and on our ability to relax. This chapter will *quieten* you on the inside, so you then start to *appreciate quiet* on the outside.

But it's hard to achieve, especially when we're beating ourselves up with this negative self-chatter. I know how Julie feels. Honestly, sometimes this voice in my own head won't shut up. But it's got a lot better. Read on and I'll tell you how.

Eckhart Tolle wrote the popular book called *The Power of Now*. He says:

'Your mind is making too much noise.'

Very often we're surrounded by noise all day long. But even when we do find a moment of quiet, many of us – like Julie – have such strong internal chatter that it's as noisy as ever. Often, it's not external silence we need; it's relief from our internal voice.

The chattering monkey

Buddhists call your internal voice 'the chattering monkey'. The chattering monkey sits on your shoulder and talks all day, and it's not very helpful:

'You can't do that.' 'You shouldn't do this.'
'That won't work.'

The chattering monkey will come up with the worst possible outcomes to events, and make damn sure he's let you know about it.

If your internal voice was positive and happy and came up with loads of great suggestions, that would be great, wouldn't it? Unfortunately, for many of us, it's not really like that. It can be unhelpful, cause stress, de-motivate, and even stop us from going to sleep.

To appreciate the power of silence, our pesky internal voice has to be a bit quieter too. So, if your mind is 'making too much noise', this chapter will show you how you can turn it down, laugh at it, ignore it, end up barely able to hear it and then make it quiet whenever you need.

Turn it down

We can change the way that we experience our internal voice. After all, it's only in our mind. If it's in our imagination, we can use our imagination to turn it down. Here's how:

>> *Listen to your internal voice. Be aware of its tone, volume, speed and pitch. The exact way that it sounds.*

>> *Imagine you have a large volume knob up there in your mind. Grab it and turn it down. That's right, start to turn your internal voice all the way down, until it gets to 1, and then, switch off.*

>> *Enjoy the silence. (1 minute)*

I know – it sounds quite simple, doesn't it? And it is. It just takes a bit of practice at first. Learn to play with the volume on your internal voice. Take charge of it.

Move it away

Another thing that works for many people is changing the space their internal voice occupies. My internal voice is just behind my right ear. I don't know why. It just is.

Where's yours? Is it behind your head? Inside your head?

Right in front of your face? In one ear, or both? Is it the 'chattering monkey' on your shoulder?

▶▶ *Work out where your internal voice is.*

▶▶ *Wherever it is, imagine moving it to a completely different place, and push it away from you. Put it behind you, or to the side, or anywhere different, and then push it away from your body.*

▶▶ *Notice how it sounds when it is further away. How much quieter is it? And smaller? Push it further away, and notice how that feels. Take charge of it. (1 minute)*

Change it

This technique works slightly differently in that it alters the way that the internal voice sounds, and puts the things it is saying into perspective. This is many people's favourite.

▶▶ *Listen to your internal voice.*

▶▶ *Turn the voice into a cartoon character's voice. Perhaps you'll go for Homer Simpson. Or Mickey Mouse. Whatever voice works, and sounds appropriately silly.*

▶▶ *Notice how inconsequential your voice sounds when it is coming from Homer, Mickey, etc., and how this gives you a different perspective on what you/they are saying. (1 minute)*

Someone I know turned her internal voice into the voice of Paris Hilton. And she told me that listening to Paris coming up with her negative self-talk was a good way of making her realise how silly it all was. Do whatever works for you.

Grab it!

Some innovative personal development coaches such as NLP (Neuro-Linguistic Programming) trainer Eric Robbie recommend a technique called the tongue grab. He says it works because the mind and body are interlinked, and we make tiny muscle movements in the mouth when we're talking to ourselves. This is what to do:

▸▸ *Take hold of your tongue. Do it gently, but firmly.*

▸▸ *Wait a little, and notice what happens. (Up to 1 minute)*

▸▸ *You may well find you become quiet inside.*

Do I make tiny muscle movements when I'm talking to myself? I've absolutely no idea. But my inner voice is quiet when I do this technique.

Grabbing the tongue can obviously be a pretty powerful message to the mind. And it's very useful to appreciate the connection between body and mind. But obviously it's not entirely practical to walk around holding your tongue all day. Some coaches recommend pushing the tongue to the top of the mouth against the teeth (to stop the movement of the tongue). However, I don't find that works as well as simply grabbing it. If it does work for you in private, and you can start to quieten that maddening mental chit-chat, then you can find that inner stillness and deep relaxation. And you'll just have to accept that you're going to look very bizarre if you 'grab it' in public!

I've already said that I have a very strong internal voice. It's always chattering on. Even after years of studying these strategies, I still have to work to keep it under control, but it does get better with practice. You've lived with your inner voice all your life, so keep going with these techniques, and you'll gradually start to take charge of your internal voice. But remember that it is important to work at this.

Relax, reflect, recharge

Now we've quietened the inner voice down, we can appreciate the value of silence. There is a famous Buddhist quote, which is also a great put-down:

Do not speak – unless it improves on silence.

The importance of silence and meditation in staying calm is well documented. Do the following techniques once a day and you may be surprised by how much more relaxed you are in certain situations. I don't recommend doing this technique at night, however. This is because I find it helps me to relax so deeply that I then feel very alert and refreshed afterwards, like I've had a good sleep. It's up to you when you do this, but I think it is best used in the morning or in the middle of the day. The first step is Relax.

Relax

1   *Ensure you are sitting somewhere quiet.*

2   *Take this minute of silence to notice how you are feeling, and make any adjustments so that your whole body is as relaxed as it can be.*

Start at your toes, and feet, and move slowly all the way up the body. Is everything as relaxed as it can be? Are you sitting comfortably? Are all the muscles in your face as relaxed as possible? Make any adjustments as necessary for the full minute, running a full check right up and down your body. (1 minute)

Reflect

1 *Say this to yourself, 'I'd like to ask my unconscious mind to reflect on any situations in the last 24 hours when I could have been more relaxed.'*

2 *Then, just sit. Odd sensation, isn't it? Sitting doing nothing. Do you feel like you should be doing something? That is why it works. You might find you consciously think about those situations, or you may find that you think about nothing at all. Either is fine.* (1 minute)

Top audiobook author Dr Stephen Simpson works as a psychologist for some of the world's top sportspeople and is also a good friend. He coaches high-achieving athletes to stay *totally* still and silent for ten seconds before a crucial situation. He says it works wonders and creates an 'inner silence'. When you 'Reflect' and 'Recharge', you're getting a whole minute – six times as long as the sports stars do!

Recharge

1 *Now shut your eyes.*

2 *Ask your 'unconscious mind' to think about three instances in the next 24 hours where you can take action to be calmer.*

3 *Just sit, with your eyes shut. Hopefully you're starting to get more used to sitting quietly. You might find that you consciously think about those situations, or you may find that you think about nothing at all. Either is fine. (1 minute)*

After doing this you can feel more focused, awake, clear, present, attuned, 'in touch' and calm.

Some people find that during Recharge, their internal voice starts to take over. That's fine. The more you use the internal voice exercises first, the better you'll get at achieving that inner stillness and quiet.

Julie was somebody who'd always had a lot of negative internal chatter, and was sceptical that she could do anything about it. It turned out (like many people who have a strong internal voice) that she responds very well to external silence, as well as turning the inner voice down. She started off by moving her internal voice away. I asked her where and she told me, 'Behind a door.' When I asked her why she said that it sounded muffled and hard to hear when she shut the door.

Then she started Relax, Reflect, Recharge. She loved the idea of appreciating the silence, but at first she was very open with me and said that she simply didn't think it worked. She noticed that the internal voice started up again. But the more she did it, and the more she practised, the more she became capable of controlling her inner voice and her responses to it.

Remember – each technique is powerful and takes one minute. And the more that you use them, the better they work.

TO-DO LIST – REMINDERS

▶▶ **To appreciate the power of silence, our internal voice has to be quieter too. Use all the techniques – Turn it down, Move it away, Change it and Grab it, and see what works best in diminishing the power of that negative self-chatter.** (Each technique 1 minute)

▶▶ *Relax* **somewhere quiet. Ensure that every part of your body is totally relaxed.** (1 minute)

▶▶ *Reflect* **somewhere quiet. Ask your 'unconscious mind' to reflect on how you could have been more relaxed in the last 24 hours. Then just be quiet. Trust yourself to work it out at a deep level.** (1 minute)

▶▶ *Recharge*: **Shut your eyes and think about three instances in the next 24 hours when you can be more relaxed.** (1 minute)

CHAPTER THREE

Calm

Tom was scared of needles. When he thought about needles, it made him feel hot, nervous, panicky and sweaty. He didn't even like being in the same room as needles. The thought of one going near him made his throat feel tight and he thought if he did ever have to be injected by one he might have a panic attack.

This was a serious problem for Tom as he is an international sportsman. In the past he had been asked to go to a prestigious tournament in Malaysia. And he actually pulled out of travelling to the tournament because he was so petrified about the prospect of having to get the correct injections for going to Asia.

So, this phobia had got to the stage where his career was being affected. It also affected other areas of his life – including going to the dentist, which left him feeling just as scared.

He knew to others it seemed irrational, but he hadn't found any techniques to actually help him deal with it.

An intense physical feeling of any kind of stress is really unpleasant. For some people that might even turn into a panic attack. If the physical symptoms you suffer are very serious, your first stop should be a doctor. But the techniques in this chapter will have an instant and powerful effect on reducing the unpleasant feelings.

We'll start with some effective breathing techniques, move on to reducing the physical symptoms and then finish with something truly powerful to get your mind thinking about the past in a different way.

Sofa Breathing

This is very effective if you are somebody who sometimes gets that tight, unpleasant, physical sensation of nerves or stress. You set it up when you're feeling relaxed. Then use it when you need it most.

I know that many people's instant reaction to 'breathing exercises' is to roll their eyes and say, 'Here we go'. I can hear you now. 'Not another hippy breathing exercise. I'm breathing already. How can this possibly help?' I know it doesn't necessarily *sound* like the most powerful of exercises. But it *is*. Have a go and see what you think.

1 *Next time you're on your sofa (or in your most comfy chair), and feeling nice and relaxed, pay full attention to your breathing. What's going on? How deep are your breaths? What pace and tempo? What position are you sitting in/standing in? What is the ratio of breathing in to breathing out? How long are you taking on the in-breath? And on the out-breath?*

Make sure to notice every aspect of your breathing in this relaxed time. (1 minute)

2 *The next time you're feeling anxious, or nervous, remember how you breathe when you're nice and relaxed. Start breathing at the same rate, pace and tempo. Find a chair/sofa/ somewhere to sit, and get in that same comfy sofa position. Now breathe in exactly the same way as you were when you were relaxed. (1 minute)*

3 *After this minute, notice how your breathing starts to become more regular and helps to lead you into a more positive state.*

Notice how the unpleasant physical feelings start to change as soon as you concentrate on your Sofa Breathing.

Breathing by Numbers

Have you ever heard of Bikram yoga? This is when the room is heated to 43°C (110°F) and a group of sweaty yoga devotees do an hour-and-a-half of bending and stretching. The heat can be quite overwhelming, which is why the teachers tell newcomers the goal is only to remain in the room for the session, even if they just sit on the floor. I recommend Bikram or 'hot yoga' as a good way to relax as well as regulate weight and metabolism.

My friend Emma came with me to hot yoga once and absolutely hated it. In fact she had to leave after about twenty minutes. She said to me afterwards, 'It's all very well the teachers telling us to stay in the room. But it was so hot I felt like I was having a panic attack and couldn't breathe.'

Emma is a pretty determined character though, and wanted to go back, so I told her about this breathing technique.

1 *Take deep breaths in and out through the nose. Deep breathing on its own promotes relaxation and calm.*

2 *Count backwards from the number 20,000. Like this: 20,000. 19,999, 19,998, 19,997, 19,996, etc. The breaths don't have to match the counting.*

3 *As you count, keep focusing on your breathing. (1 minute)*

4 *If you lose your place or get the numbers wrong, go back to 20,000 and start your minute again.*

It is surprisingly hard to focus on the numbers, and get it right. This is good – the change in focus is important. It's all about putting your attention in an utterly different place.

Emma went back to hot yoga. Using this breathing technique, she eventually stayed for the whole session on her third attempt. Taking her focus away from the heat and on to counting backwards was enough to make the class bearable. She was quite exhilarated afterwards, and said to me, 'I never imagined I'd be able to stay in the room that long, although I didn't realise how bad I was at counting backwards.'

Virtual Massage

A good massage is always worth it for the effect it has on our physical and mental well-being. They're expensive though, aren't they? I'm always shocked at the price of a massage and

I reckon most of us can't afford more than the occasional one as a treat.

So instead I present to you – the Virtual Massage. It's very comforting. And I've saved you lots of cash at the same time. This is especially good if you are somebody who responds well to touch and are sometimes referred to as a 'touchy-feely' or 'physical' person. Use it any time you want to feel more comfortable.

1 *Imagine a small, warm, glowing orb in front of your forehead. It is the perfect temperature, warm without being hot. Notice what colour it is, and how it feels pleasant when it just touches your forehead.*

2 *You are in control of the orb, so roll it slowly across your forehead, gently massaging it with warmth, along the contours of your face, and then very lightly rubbing and warming each temple.*

3 *Now guide it slowly, moving to the back of your neck. Roll it slowly up and down the spine of your neck, feeling yourself filling with a lovely warmth and relaxation. Guide the orb to apply gentle pressure and warmth to each shoulder, massaging and relaxing and releasing all tension. Feel the healing warmth spreading right through your shoulders and back.*

4 *Gently but firmly move the orb to any part of your body where you feel physical stress. Make sure you gently massage it with warmth, and notice the pleasant, relaxing feeling you get.*

5 *If any thoughts pop into your mind while you're doing this, that's OK. Just acknowledge them, and carry on. (1 minute)*

Why does this work so well? Well the mind and body are completely interlinked. By letting go of physical tension, your more relaxed body starts to have an impact on your mental state as well.

The Rock Star Phobia Cure

Use this if you've had a particularly bad experience with nerves or stress at some point in your past. If you've had any kind of seriously upsetting experience that makes you feel anxious, do this. It is common for people to be held back by a bad memory, and this technique can work well to counter its effects. Make sure to start it at a time beforehand when you felt safe and relaxed.

This is inspired by the countless rock stars who've thrown TVs out of hotel windows. If only all those rock stars had followed my technique and done it *in their minds*, they would have saved themselves a big bill, as well as perhaps getting over some of their rock star hang-ups.

It is an updated version of The Window technique that I used in my book *Confidence in a Minute*, with a new, powerful ending.

1 *Imagine you are sitting in the corner of a large hotel room and you can see yourself sitting on the bed watching a small black-and-white TV in the opposite corner to you. (So – it's you, watching yourself – watching the screen.)*

2 *Watch yourself watching the negative experience – with nerves or stress – in black and white. Watch it through in black and white. Finish it on pause at another time afterwards – any*

time at all – when, again, you felt safe and relaxed.

3   *Now imagine yourself clambering into the black and white screen, so you are now in the picture, stuck in the safe and relaxed moment you just paused.*

4   *Make your surroundings colour. Start to rewind, so that it rewinds in colour around you. Ensure that, in a few seconds, you are paused back at the start again.* *(1 minute)*

If at any point this feels uncomfortable, step out of the picture again, return to your position in the corner and make the black and white TV picture fuzzy and blurry.

1   *Now, go back to the corner in your imagination and repeat this process. (Remember, you go forward in black and white, and backwards in colour.)* *(1 minute)*

2   *Repeat again, but this time the black and white screen is more and more fuzzy. This hotel TV has seriously dodgy reception.* *(1 minute)*

3   *Repeat again, and this time the TV in the corner is much smaller, and the reception even worse. Make sure the sound on the hotel TV remote control is switched to mute. (Remember, you are still watching yourself sitting on the bed watching the small TV right over in the corner.)* *(1 minute)*

4   *Repeat the above, making the TV smaller. Keep repeating until you feel that the negative emotions surrounding the event have become more neutral emotions. That's what you want. You don't have to look back and love the memory. You can just feel more neutral about it.* *(Each repetition – 1 minute)*

5 And now the rock star bit. Do this as soon as the emotions feel more neutral. Watch yourself switch off the TV with the remote and walk over and pick the TV up. It is surprisingly light and easy to carry. You walk over to the window, open it, check nobody is underneath the window (this is important), and throw the TV out of the window. That particular TV is not going to work again.

The black-and-white TV makes it harder for you to associate with the negative emotions surrounding your previous episode. The colour rewind scrambles and confuses the way your brain thinks about the episode. And throwing the TV out of the window means that particular memory will never work in quite the same way again. You'll find the memories are still there but they don't hold the same power over you that they once did.

It turned out that when Tom was eleven years old, he'd had an unpleasant experience at the dentist with needles, and ever since, this had had an impact on how he thought about them. He had to get it sorted this time though.

He did the Rock Star Phobia Cure, and before we started I asked him to rate his fear out of 10. He said, 'Nine'. I ran the Rock Star Phobia Cure once. Just once. And I asked him how he rated that fear now. Straight away he said 'Four'. We ran it again. He squinted, as if he couldn't see the picture. He said, 'Maybe a two…'. Then he threw the old TV out of the imaginary window (remembering to check that the imaginary ground below the imaginary window was clear first).

Tom finally got over his phobia of needles using the Rock Star technique. Now, he doesn't exactly like getting the injections he needs to fly to exotic destinations, but he feels more comfortable and neutral about it. He also uses the breathing techniques to help him. He says he's got very good at counting backwards, and he is now able to fly all over the world to compete.

TO-DO LIST – REMINDERS

▶▶ *Sofa Breathing:* Next time you're on your sofa (or in your most comfy chair), and feeling really nice and relaxed, pay full attention to your breathing. Then when you feel stressed out, you can replicate this lovely, relaxed breathing. (1 minute)

▶▶ *Breathing by Numbers:* As you breathe deeply, count backwards from the number 20,000. Like this: 20,000. 19,999. 19,998, 19,997, 19,996, etc. If you lose your place, start the minute again. The way this technique fully occupies the mind seems to work really well for many people. (1 minute)

▶▶ *The Virtual Massage:* This will save you shelling out ten times the price of this book on one massage! Gently but firmly guide your warm, imaginary orb around any and all areas of your body where you feel physical stress, and notice how you start to relax as you follow the instructions. (1 minute)

▶▶ *The Rock Star Phobia Cure:* If you've had any kind of seriously upsetting experience in the past, start to change the way you think about it. It is common for people to be held back by a bad memory, and they often find this technique very helpful. (1 minute per run-through)

CHAPTER FOUR

Sleep

Tina's first feeling on waking up was often one of 'absolute disgust' that she'd not had enough sleep. She admitted to me, 'I'm not sure absolute disgust is the best way to start the day.'

She was lucky if she got six hours' sleep a night. She was always busy, and often didn't even seem to have eight hours left in the day to actually shut her eyes and get some sleep. But even more than that, once she turned the light out, her mind would race with all her worries and problems, and it would regularly take her hours to get to sleep. She'd think about her relationships, her work and her age, and she'd end up feeling utterly awake – and depressed.

Because she was so tired, her caffeine intake was high – on average ten caffeinated drinks a day. She made a flask of tea when she left the house in the morning, and started drinking from it on the drive to work. By the time she arrived she'd had three cups already, and she

desperately needed a pee! She knew she was consuming too much caffeine, but she had to get through the day somehow.

This chapter will help you to sleep longer and deeper, which will have an overall benefit on your entire health and well-being, as well as your ability to relax. We also look at the 'half-life' of caffeine – the time required for the body to get rid of one half of the total amount of the caffeine swilling around in it. There are four parts to this chapter:

1 *Getting to sleep*

2 *Sleep deeper*

3 *The next morning*

4 *Eight hours' sleep in 30 seconds?*

But first, the stats. In his book *Counting Sheep*, sleep expert Paul Martin details the frankly terrifying list of consequences of not sleeping enough: you can become anxious or sad. Your body temperature goes down. Your levels of stress hormones go up. You're more likely to get spots, become flabby, come down with flu and become depressed. Sex drive can go down. Blood pressure can go up. You're more at risk of a heart attack and a stroke. And, you're more likely to have a road accident. (Apparently sleep-related road accidents can be easily identified because there are no tyre skid marks.)

If you're somebody who finds it hard to relax in certain areas, it might be that sleep is a good place to start, as some people say part of the reason they get so stressed is because they simply can't get a good night's sleep. There's nothing worse than going to bed and wanting to sleep but being awake. It is 2 a.m., you switched out the light three hours ago, and for some reason you're thinking in intricate detail about the laundry you've got to do tomorrow. Very stressful.

So how much sleep is a good amount? There doesn't seem to be one agreed-upon figure. But I quite like this definition from Professor Jim Horne of Loughborough University's Sleep Research Centre: 'The amount of sleep we require is what we need not to be sleepy in the daytime.'

This chapter looks at simple techniques that take only a minute and which start to rewire your brain throughout the day for a deep, relaxed, good night's sleep. Don't miss out on eight hours' sleep when it means you could be feeling refreshed and revitalised.

One more thing. If you've got small children, you may well be thinking – 'How on earth is he going to find more time for me to sleep?' I admit, children are extraordinarily talented at hoovering up our sleep time. But as you read on, you'll discover that it's not just about the *length* of time you sleep, it's also the *quality* of sleep, how *deeply* you sleep, how *quickly* you are able to drop off and also how you *wake up* in the morning.

Getting to sleep 1: Get some Zzzzzs

Many people say it's not that they don't allow enough time for sleep, it's just that when they actually get into bed, their mind starts racing. And then they feel more awake and alert than they have all day.

We've all had this at some point. When we eventually turn the light out, it's often the first time all day we've had to do something really important, and that is to be quiet and think. One of the secrets of getting to sleep in these circumstances is to prepare for sleep in the right way. In the moments before you drop off, it's not helpful to be thinking of all the problems that await you the next morning. It's better to clear your mind to prepare for a deep rest, and you do this by using the senses of sight, sound and feeling to occupy the mind.

When you are ready for sleep, work out how many hours you'd like to sleep for. This number is important and I'll refer to it as 'Z' in the technique. If you want eight hours' sleep, then Z = 8. If you have set the alarm for six hours, then Z = 6. If you want to sleep for six-and-a-half hours, then round it up so Z = 7. And make sure you set an alarm.

So just to be clear, when Z is referred to in this technique, it refers to the number of hours you're going to sleep for. Now, let's get some Zzzzzs:

1 *Be still. Notice (Z) things that you can see. Go slowly, concentrating on every one.*

2 *Notice (Z) things that you can hear. Again, go slowly.*

3 *Now notice (Z) things that you can feel or touch. For example, it might be the temperature of the air, the duvet on your back, the feeling of the sheet against your skin.*

4 *Now shut your eyes and continue the process, seeing in your mind (Z) things in the room you could previously see. Notice (Z) things you can hear, and (Z) things you can feel. (1 minute)*

If your mind wanders, start the full minute again. This is important. Once you manage a full minute of this, it will usually be enough to take you into a nice, relaxed, different state. From there, you'll find you are mentally prepared for sleep. But you must complete the full minute.

By fully occupying your mind, it can't concentrate on all the stuff that it was mulling over. That distraction takes you into a different place, ready for sleep. And then the repetition of counting out the number of hours you want to sleep for gives your mind some powerful unconscious suggestions.

HINT

■ Where people often go wrong with this technique is that they don't do it for the full minute. Their mind starts wandering much sooner, sometimes even after a few seconds. When you do this for a full minute, your mind will be in a different place, ready for sleep.

Getting to sleep 2: Audio help

My friend John responds really well to listening. He loves music, and 'the sound of things', and listening to the radio. He could listen to it for ten hours a day. He is clearly somebody who responds a lot better to listening to stuff than reading. Many people do.

You might be somebody who responds better to listening to something before bed, rather than reading this or concentrating on something else. In this instance, you might do well to invest in a sleep audio download, and put it on before you go to bed. There are plenty out there. One of them is my audio program – iSleep. You can get it on my website www.tonywrighton.com or on iTunes. Read the reviews and see what people say about how it does the job of occupying the mind for them.

Sleep deeper

Experts say that the quality of your sleep is often more important than how long you sleep for. How 'deeply' you sleep is a crucial factor. And a lack of deep sleep can affect every other area of your life.

Caffeine

Did you know that the average 'half-life' of caffeine is six hours or more? That means that if you have a cup of coffee at 4 p.m., at 10 p.m. half of it is still swilling around your body. And at 4 a.m. (twelve hours later), you've still got the effects of a quarter of a cup of coffee working away on your body and mind.

Remember Tina? She was drinking up to ten cups of tea a day. No wonder she couldn't get to sleep. Even when it didn't stop her getting to sleep, on the above calculations, the caffeine would impair her ability to sleep deeply.

The problem is that caffeine is in a lot of things that we tend to enjoy – tea, coffee, fizzy drinks, chocolate, even decaf coffee! I'm not saying you should give all that up (although some experts do advise it). I'm suggesting a small change first, to see if it works for you. It is one put forward by sleep expert Daniel Kripke of the University of California, who advises 'not to drink or eat anything caffeinated within six hours of bedtime'.

This is about becoming more aware of the effect caffeine has on you. When you don't have caffeine, how does it affect the quality of your sleep? The more aware you are of what works for you, the more you can control a great night's sleep.

Temperature

Research shows that body temperature is closely linked to how well and how deeply we sleep. That is why we're often quite restless on a hot summer's night. And, of course, why it can be hard to sleep if we're too cold. A group of researchers from the Australasian sleep foundation conducted a huge survey on sleep patterns, and they found:

To drop off we must cool off; body temperature and the brain's sleep–wake cycle are closely linked. The blood flow mechanism that transfers core body heat to the skin works best between 18 and 30 degrees. But later in life, the comfort zone shrinks to between 23 and 25 degrees – one reason why older people have more sleep disorders.

By the way, you might want to do a bit more research on the power of a warm bath before bed. One way to get your body feeling right is said to be taking a warm (but not hot) bath. Apparently it helps the body to kick-start the process of cooling down for sleep.

Spending less time in bed if you're not sleeping

A lot of the problems associated with insomnia are because people spend so much time lying in bed worrying about it. They then come to associate their bed with anxiety and bad feelings – obviously not ideal.

Daniel Kripke says the solution is to get out of bed when you're not sleepy, and restrict your time in bed. He says of people who do this:

> **They get over their fear of the bed. They get over the worry, and become confident that when they go to bed, they will sleep. So spending less time in bed actually makes sleep better. It is in fact a more powerful and effective long-term treatment for insomnia than sleeping pills.**

And now, let me ask you a question. Do you have a TV in the bedroom, for example, or a laptop? You might want to move that TV into another room. As health and well-being author Dr Frank Lipman says, 'There are only two things you should do in bed, and they both begin with the letter S.' (Although presumably not at the same time?)

The next morning

Tina told me that her first feeling on waking up was one of 'absolute disgust'.

We decided to change those first few moments, so I asked if I could have a look at her alarm clock. Tina brought it in, and gave me a little demo. BEEP! BEEP! BEEP! BEEP! It was horrible. It sounded like a fire alarm or an emergency warning sound.

We got rid of the nuclear warning zone alarm clock and instead set an alarm on her phone with a song from her music library.

Tina said the moment her alarm went off the next day, she started laughing. It was just such a chilled way to start the day. What did she pick? James Brown's *I Feel Good*, which is a pretty positive message to start the day with. Tina couldn't physically find more hours to sleep, but she could change the way she started the day.

> *Do away with that hideous 'beep, beep, beep' alarm clock you've been using for years, and start the day as you mean to go on. On most phones you can now customise your alarm with any music you like. Set your alarm with a favourite relaxing song, or cheery and uplifting song – whatever you prefer – and then notice how it changes the way you feel when you wake up in the morning. (1 minute)*

If this isn't possible, get an alarm that starts quietly and slowly increases in volume, or one of those posh ones that plays a CD. It's the first moment of your day. Why not make it a good moment?

Incidentally, sleep author Paul Martin is not keen on conventional alarms at all, and instead suggests a modern device designed to simulate dawn in the bedroom by gradually increasing the intensity of light over the half-hour before you want to wake up.

Eight hours' sleep in 30 seconds?

We've already spoken about the calming and restorative benefits of yoga. There is a yoga pose that some respected teachers claim is the equivalent of eight hours' sleep. I've always been slightly sceptical of this claim. Wouldn't we all have lots more time to do stuff if we could get sleep out of the way in 30 seconds?

But I must admit that the pose known as Ardha Kurmasana or 'Half Tortoise' is very relaxing, and is also said to help with insomnia. Do this if you want to feel refreshed during the day, or if you're lying in bed at night and struggling to get to sleep. It might not leave you feeling like you've had eight hours' sleep. But it might . . .

1 *Get down on your knees and sit on your heels. (If this is uncomfortable then this exercise probably isn't for you.)*

2 *Straighten your arms above you so they touch your ears and bring your hands together, interlocking only your thumbs.*

3 *Slowly bend forward with your arms straight until your little fingers touch the floor, then your forehead. Use your abdominal muscles for strength and stability as you go down. Try to keep your bottom on your heels (not easy).*

4 *Stay in this pose, with your forehead on the ground, and your little fingers too. Hold it for around 30 seconds – or longer if you so desire – and then slowly reverse the whole exercise, returning your still straight arms and body to vertical. Bring your arms down. (1 minute)*

Ardha Kurmasana or 'Half Tortoise' pose

This position stretches the spine, massages the internal organs, helps with indigestion and digestion, and relaxes the brain with a fresh supply of blood.

This is calming to do at any time of the day. I also find that getting into this position in bed can be relaxing. By all means combine this technique with the 'Getting to sleep' technique. Don't worry how you look. If it feels good and relaxing, that's good enough.

Schedule in enough sleep

One more thing. Are you actually scheduling yourself enough sleep? There's no easy solution to this one. Unfortunately there's no magic pill to create another three hours in the middle of the night. But if your answer to this question is no, is there any way you can schedule in more time for sleep? If you have young children, can you share child-minding duties with your other half? Can you ask somebody else to help out so you can get some extra sleep? Are you prioritising sleep as highly as other parts of your life?

Or if it's not to do with kids, can you go to bed earlier in the evening? Switch the TV off? Turn the laptop off? Put your phone on silent? And get in bed earlier? I realise this may be stating the obvious, but sometimes the obvious is worth saying. If you need any more motivation to plan a little more sleep for yourself, please go back and read the paragraph at the start of this chapter about the effects of not getting enough sleep.

Back to Tina. After she changed her alarm clock, we looked at her caffeine-drinking habits. She'd been drinking tea for so long (and loved it so much) that she didn't want to totally give it up. So she agreed to not have any within six hours of bedtime. That helped – a lot.

But what she loved most was the 'Getting to sleep' exercise. She had been going to sleep and running through all her problems in her mind at that late stage of the day. Now she cleared her mind before sleep and more often than not, after one minute of doing this, she was 'chilled out enough to drop off'. That's what you want.

TO-DO LIST – REMINDERS

▸▸ *Getting to sleep 1:* The secret of getting to sleep is to prepare your mind for it. Forget about your day and start to relax by occupying your mind with your present surroundings, stuff you can see/hear/feel. If distracted, start again until you can do this for the entire minute. (1 minute)

▸▸ *Getting to sleep 2:* Many people respond excellently to listening to something before bed. If this is the case for you, invest in a sleep audio download, and then switch on in the minute before you want to go to sleep. (Switch on before sleep – a few seconds. Then just listen)

▸▸ *Sleeping deeper:* Think about your caffeine intake, the temperature in the room and how much 'non-sleep' time you spend in bed. Can you make changes in order to sleep deeper at night?

▸▸ *The next morning:* Do away with that loud beep, beep, beep alarm clock you've been using for years, and start the day as you mean to go on. Set your alarm with a favourite relaxing song, or an upbeat one if you prefer. Then notice how it changes the way you feel when you wake up in the morning. (1 minute to set)

▸▸ *Eight hours' sleep in 30 seconds:* This is the claim by yoga teachers for the 'Half Tortoise' pose. Is it true? Get into the position and try it, and see whether you feel like you've had eight hours' sleep, or perhaps you simply feel more relaxed and calm. (30 seconds)

CHAPTER FIVE

Simplify

'Fifteen emails sent overnight? Do people never rest?'

Olivia always felt like she was playing catch-up. She was constantly on the go and never felt like she had enough time in the day. Early in the morning it took her about an hour to clear her inbox. During the day, she'd try and grab five or ten minutes whenever she could to keep managing the emails. She even found herself checking her emails on her phone last thing at night and first thing in the morning. She never had enough time. In any one day, Olivia would send around fifty messages. It was overwhelming. Mind you, she also found time during the day to make at least fifteen phone calls, watch TV (or sometimes just be aware of the TV on in the background), listen to the radio at work, surf her favourite websites, read her favourite online food blogs, use apps on her phone, send texts, listen to her iPod and more.

As a result, her train of thought was constantly being distracted. She'd be writing a paper and then an email

would come in, she would answer it, read a link within it, click on something else and, before she knew it, fifteen minutes had gone and she'd lost her original train of thought completely. The same applied at home. She'd be trying to do one thing, and her train of thought would be so distracted that she'd realise she was all of a sudden looking at a picture of her ex's best friend's wife's new puppy.

Olivia needed practical, specific help in how to manage her life more effectively, because at the moment she just felt overwhelmed.

Are you suffering from information overload? Can the technology sometimes be a bit too much? This is the age of extreme information, where the latest Ofcom (the UK communications regulator) research suggests we are connected to information (email, text, social networking, TV, radio) for on average at least seven hours a day.

So it's time to simplify. This chapter will help you to:

>> *simplify life*

>> *make specific changes to reduce distractions and get more done.*

This in turn will help you to:

>> *get stuff done quicker*

>> *relax.*

The theme of simplifying life pops up again and again in historical teachings. The nineteenth-century American author and philosopher Henry David Thoreau said:

Our life is frittered away by detail.
Simplify, simplify, simplify!

And the Chinese Taoist philosopher Lao Tzu said:

Simple in actions and in thoughts,
you return to the source of being.

Simplicity is a theme that has been around for many centuries and, because of modern technology, we need to work harder to simplify than ever before. Our mission: to make the technology work for us, not against us.

Doing one thing at a time

The benefits of doing one thing at a time are huge. By putting more focus, effort and energy into each thing you do throughout the day, you'll get it done quicker and better, *and* you'll find you have more time for the other things you were attempting to multi-task at the same time. You'll become more fully present and engaged in the moment of what you are doing.

You may well be very good at eating your dinner, sending people messages on the internet, talking to your other half and watching the TV all at the same time. But you might find that when you do each of those things individually, you get more satisfaction and productivity from each one. You are more present. You appreciate things more. You devote all your energy to each thing you do. Your mind is clearer.

Making sure you actually do one thing at a time

Here's the thing. At the moment, I don't *trust* you (or myself) to actually do one thing at a time. I know we have the right intentions. But I also know what human nature is like. I know what I'm like. We'll think this is a great idea, and then all of a sudden we'll catch ourselves checking our work emails on our phone in the bathroom, while trying to clean our teeth and listen to the radio, and writing tonight's shopping list while juggling a laptop and attempting to make an important phone call.

Happily, I have a way to use the technology to give us a constant reminder of this particular goal:

1 *Get a piece of paper, and write the words* 'One thing at a time' *on it.*

2 *Take a photo of it.*

3 *Set it as your screensaver and desktop wallpaper on your computer, and as your lock screen and home screen on your phone. Then pin the piece of paper on the wall for good measure. (1 minute)*

This works because the modern technology is ensuring you see your goal at very regular intervals throughout the day. It also works because we're more likely to do something when it is written down. If you don't have a mobile phone that is capable of doing this, congratulations, life is probably already a little bit simpler for you.

I have played around with the words written on the piece of paper, and you can too, if you like. For instance, one day I realised I'd been on my phone aimlessly social networking and unnecessarily checking emails for an hour-and-a-quarter. I grabbed a piece of paper and wrote in large letters:

REALLY?

That photo then became my screensaver, and acted as an effective reminder. Did I REALLY need to be opening my phone again, when I could be savouring the present?

Now that's set up, here are some other suggestions for simplifying your life, and doing one thing at a time.

The 0.07 commitment

For many, email and internet are the bane of working life. They can consume so much time that hours need to be set aside to deal with replying to emails and surfing the net. It ends up being stressful, and relentless. The information overload contributes to this stress. A lot of people will be reading this and thinking – yes! For others it simply won't be relevant. (My mum only checks her email once every three days. She doesn't need an email strategy.)

If this is relevant to you, the 0.07 commitment will help you create a lot more time for yourself with an email and internet plan.

I'm asking you to spend 0.07 per cent of your day ensuring that you approach it in the right manner and stick to your goal of simplifying and doing one thing at a time. (In case you hadn't realised, 0.07 per cent of your day is one minute. That's not much, is it?)

1   *Before you start the important and productive part of your day (work, errands, meetings, looking after children), sit for one uninterrupted minute.*

2   *Write a brief plan for when you are going to 'do emails'. For instance, 'I will check emails at 11 a.m., 1 p.m., 3 p.m. and 5 p.m.' Or, 'I will check emails when I arrive at work, at lunchtime, and before I leave.'*

3   *Write down a separate time for personal web-surfing. For instance, 'I will do personal web stuff between 8 and 9 p.m. tonight. For the rest of the day, I'll use the web for work only.'*
    (1 minute to make plan = 0.07 per cent of the day)

It's as simple to simplify as that. Once you've made the plan, and written it down, you're more likely to stick to it. Then you'll find it's easier to simplify your actions, simplify your thoughts and do one thing at a time.

Are you wondering if this is possible with your current job? Read on.

Email off

You know that little 'ding' sound on your computer when you receive an email? And the minimised display telling you how many unread emails you have? And the tiny pop-up box with 'new email'? File all this under 'distractions'. It all adds to our information overload. We can have the best of intentions not to get distracted, but these things still do sidetrack us.

We are now on a mission to get rid of unnecessary information:

> *Switch off email when you are working on something non-email related. Switch off at all times when not scheduled to be checking. (5 seconds to switch off, plenty more time to devote to everything else)*

When you do this, you might be surprised at how much less stressful your list of tasks seems. And how much clearer your other tasks seem to be.

I realise that, for some people, in some jobs, this may not be possible. In which case, build yourself in more frequent windows for checking email. Even if you're only switching off the email for a few minutes at a time at first, these small changes will make a big difference to you. And you can still simplify more:

> *Switch off any email sound effects and pop-ups. Do this on all devices that receive email. (1 minute)*

> *Switch off the 'dock unread count'. This is the tiny number that tells you how many unread emails you have in the corner of the screen, even when you're not in that window. (1 minute)*

This second change has made a big difference to me at times when my email is open, because my eyes don't idly wander to the little red 'unread emails' sign every five seconds.

It's about making sure to simplify as much as possible.

Tell people about your email habits

Author Tim Ferriss wrote *The 4-Hour Work Week*. He's an interesting person, not least because he seems to spend most of his time tango-dancing in Buenos Aires or diving in

Panama while his successful business carries on effortlessly without him.

He has written about the problem of information overload, and this suggestion comes from his blog at www.fourhourworkweek.com

> ▶▶ *Try an email signature that reads 'I answer email at 10 a.m., 1 p.m. and 4 p.m. If you need a quicker response, please call.'*

Incidentally, Tim Ferriss has now got so good at cutting email out of his life that he says he checks it once a week, for one hour. Imagine all the extra time he has to devote to other stuff. Could you ever get down to once a week, for one hour? I couldn't. But the principle behind his email signature is to cut down on email, while still maintaining important relationships.

Windows

This simplifies the space that your brain works in on a screen. It's like tidying up an office or bedroom, except you're tidying up your computer screen, and simplifying the space you work in.

1 *'Declutter' your computer by only having three windows open at any one time. This includes email, work documents, internet pages (and separate tabs within one browser), Skype, iTunes, calendar, and anything else you might have open.*

2 *If you notice you have more than three open, shut windows until there are only three. (1 minute)*

Fewer things to think about at once = Less information coming in = Doing one thing at a time = Simplify.

Headphones

You're working away on something, deep in thought and concentration, and somebody comes up to talk to you about last night's TV. It's not that you don't want to talk to them – you just don't want to talk to them right now. By the time you go back to what you were doing, you've completely lost your train of thought. It's not just the time of the interruption, it's also the time it takes to refocus on what you were doing.

I've found that nobody interrupts me when I have headphones on. There is an almost endless list of places where you can use them. At home, in the coffee shop, in a bar, or restaurant, people rarely disturb you when you're wearing headphones. (And if they do, a vaguely irritated look as you pull one earphone out should do the trick. This is the body language equivalent of saying . . . you'd better be quick.)

What about at work? You're worried your boss might not like this? Why not tell him/her exactly why you want to do it? He'd probably applaud your creativity and your desire to be more single-minded. (If you *are* the boss, have a 'headphones day' and see how much work everybody gets done.)

You don't even need to be listening to music. In fact only listen to music if you want to block out more distracting noise. This is the secondary benefit of headphones. In fact, as I write some loud roadworks have started up outside the window. I put my headphones in and some classical music on, and the distraction is blocked out. (1 minute)

Personal time

The other day I was playing football with friends. In the middle of our game, my friend's mobile phone went off. He stopped, ran over to the side of the pitch. Instead of switching it off, he answered it. 'Hello . . . Yeah . . . I'm just playing football . . . Yup . . . OK, I'll call you when I'm finished.'

This was not very relaxing for him, and not very relaxing for his team-mates either. The irony is that we sometimes allow ourselves to be distracted at the times of the week we most look forward to. He loves his football, and yet he interrupted it for a call he didn't need to take.

So maintain this focus on one thing at a time in your personal time too. Simplify. And then you'll enjoy that kickabout/hanging out with friends/going to the cinema even more.

HINT

■ This is *how not to simplify*. You wake up. You check your emails on your phone in bed before you get up. As you brush your teeth, you're listening to the radio, doing up your shoelaces and watching the TV. When you walk down the street to the station, you're checking the latest news websites on your phone or sending texts. When you arrive at work, you have multiple windows open on your computer. When a message comes in you check it, regardless of what else you

HINT *cont.*

are doing and regardless of how it affects your concentration. In the evening you go out for a drink with friends, but you keep an eye on your phone, regularly checking it for texts, emails and anything more exciting. When you get home, you browse your computer as you talk to your other half about your day.

This is *how to simplify*. You wake up. You clean your teeth, focusing solely on the brushing. When you put your shoes on, you focus only on putting your shoes on. You sit down and listen to the radio for five minutes. Then you switch it off. Then you make your breakfast. Then you eat it. Then you leave for work. As you walk down the street, you engage fully in the activity of walking down the street. When you're finally sitting on the train, you can take out your phone, and devote your full attention to the day's news, or your latest messages. At work, you do one thing at a time. You devote specific times of the day for specific tasks, such as email. You don't eat lunch at your desk, but instead go somewhere else, and focus on the food. In the evening, you go for a drink with friends. Your phone is off or on silent, so it doesn't distract you and you can really engage in the conversation. When you get home, you sit down and spend some quality time with your partner. You cook. Then you eat. You savour each part of your day. Fully present.

Olivia had a real tendency to over-burden herself with a million things at once. She was so busy; she could never relax and focus calmly on one thing at once. She started writing the 0.07 commitment every morning. After a few weeks she said, 'It's not been easy. My instinct is still to open every email, even the ones advertising bargains from my favourite online shoe shop. However, having written down in the morning when I'm going to check my emails and use the internet, that usually gives me just enough pause to stop me doing it. And I'm doing much more, and working much quicker, and have much more time to chat to people as I go. More than that though, my head feels clearer. That's a good feeling.'

TO-DO LIST – REMINDERS

We live in the age of extreme information. We need to work harder to make the technology work for us, not against us. The way to do this is by simplifying your life, doing one thing at a time, reducing the amount of information that you consume and improving the quality of that information.

▶▶ Get more done and feel more relaxed at the same time. Get a piece of paper and write 'One thing at a time' on it. Take a photo and set it as your screen-saver on your computer and mobile phone. Then pin the paper up somewhere prominent too. (1 minute)

▶▶ Devote 0.07 per cent of your day to ensuring you stick to your goal of simplifying and doing one thing at a time. Plan exactly when you will send emails and surf the web for personal use. (0.07 per cent of your day)

▶▶ Simplify your life by: switching off email when you're not using it, having only three windows open on the computer at once, using headphones to help you maintain your focus, and reducing distractions in personal time too. (All 1 minute to set up = extra hours every day)

CHAPTER SIX

Switch Off

When Simon was a child, he loved playing chess. He was a talented chess player at school, and said he enjoyed the fact that he was good at it and it was such a relaxing activity. He particularly enjoyed sitting outside in the garden and playing chess with his dad. Some of his happiest memories were sitting in the sunshine and staring intently at that chessboard, with not a care in the world apart from what his next move was going to be.

Now, Simon never played chess. And he never seemed to be able to just switch his brain off from his hectic schedule and just relax and enjoy life. Perhaps playing chess again would help him to feel more relaxed? His brain had only a few moments to mull this over before his phone beeped. A tweet! About him! He must reply. But before he had time to do this, an email came in. Ding! He checked it. Work-related. Best get that out of the way now. But as soon as he started replying, a text message arrived. Ping! The email, the tweet and the memory of playing chess in the garden with his dad were cast aside.

It didn't matter where he was, and what time of day it was, his brain was always working away, thinking about one thing or another, work-related, money-related, friends-related . . . you name it. Even when Simon went to bed he would run a last-minute email check before sleep, and even then he was thinking about possible Facebook status updates.

Simon's lifestyle was relentless, addictive and tiring.

In the previous chapter, we looked at very specific ways of managing the daily distractions in your life. In this one, we completely switch off from modern life, and it still only takes a minute.

For Simon, and many others like him, it's not necessarily the chess that would help him to relax, but focusing all his attention on any one thing to the exclusion of all else. And the evidence is that we're finding this harder than ever to do.

Writer William Leith says:

Everything around us – the phones and the clocks and the computers and the hand-held emailing devices – makes us busier. After a certain point we become overloaded.

Dr Frank Lipman has written a book on exhaustion called *Spent*. He says:

We get Spent because our modern lifestyle has removed us from nature and we have become divorced from its rhythms and cycles.

It's time to get back to basics, and get back to that enthusiastic chess-playing child in the garden again. In this chapter, you will learn to:

>> *properly 'switch off' for a few moments in the middle of the day*

>> *improve your ability to 'switch off' and relax long term*

>> *improve your attention span*

>> *appreciate really important things around you, which don't have switches.*

For the purposes of this chapter, the phrase 'switch off' of course has a useful double meaning. It refers to switching off the technology as well as enjoying a moment of personal relaxation time. And it only takes a minute to switch off.

Why is modern life making us anxious? Our grandparents never had all this incredible technology, healthcare and knowledge. Indeed, many of the techniques in this book even make great use of modern technology. Our lives should be easier and more stress-free than ever before.

But we are also cramming in more than ever before. It seems our minds need downtime to cope with all the uptime. The technology is there to help us, not control us and it is harder than ever to simply 'switch off'. In a blog for the *Guardian*'s Comment is Free website, writer and TV critic Charlie Brooker recently bemoaned the fact that in some jobs people 'spend more time gazing at screens than into the eyes of people'.

Imagine that: spending more time looking at a little flickering screen than looking into the eyes of a warm, living, breathing, exciting, unpredictable, actual person.

In an article for the *Huffington Post*, the writer and blogger Linda Stone coined a phrase, 'email apnea'. Her research has found people actually 'reduced their oxygen intake' when they checked a new email. Ok, so now we're staring at a screen all day long and holding our breath while we do it. That's worrying.

I told Simon about all this stuff, and I posed him a question.

'Are you using the technology, or is the technology using you?'

In a moment of impulse, he closed his laptop lid and switched off the power supply. Well, that went OK. He then switched off the radio, which had been warbling aimlessly in the background. He switched his phone onto silent, and then realised that wasn't really the same as switching it off, so he turned that off completely too. The TV wasn't on, but he pulled out the power supply too, just for good measure. He unplugged the telephone landline, and then . . .

He felt lost. He felt a bit naked. What might he be missing? What might be going on without him, while he was not connected to the world?

He sat down and looked out of the window. He felt that it was a strange sensation, being so aware of time passing and not doing anything about it.

And then something very odd happened. I'll tell you what exactly at the end of the chapter. But first, do the 'Switch off' exercise, and see if your experience is the same as Simon's.

Switch off

I've been doing the following exercise for years, and I hope it works as well for you as it does for me. Most of our stress comes from worrying about something that's happened or concern over something that's going to happen. This exercise is about noticing what's happening around you right now and 'being present'. It's hard to switch off at first. But it is worth it. By paying attention to your attention span, you increase its power.

1 *Switch everything off. Phone, email, internet, computer, TV, radio, iPod and anything else. (1 minute)*

2 *Look out of the window at the clouds in the sky. Focus on the cloud patterns, the swirls and their movement. Keep your attention entirely on the clouds, and noticing everything you can about the way they look. (around 1 minute – no need to keep a stopwatch on it though)*

3 *Here's the tricky part. Every time you realise that you've started thinking about something else, and lost your focus on the clouds, you have to start the full minute again. Many particularly stressed people find it takes them quite a while to actually be able to focus on just one thing. If you find you have to go back to the beginning a few times, it's just a sign that you will especially benefit from this 'switching off' technique.*

4 *Once you've done a full minute – congratulations. You are now fully in the present. There is no room for any thoughts of past or future to enter for a full minute.*

Switch whatever you need to back on. But notice any differences in how you feel.

5 *Do this once a day. Notice how you feel before and after 'switching off'.* *(1 minute daily)*

It's surprisingly hard to do this. People have said to me that it has sometimes taken them up to half-an-hour to actually 'switch off' for the full minute. It's difficult. Remember, you haven't actually completed the technique until you've focused for the full minute.

I've just 'switched off'. I had to 'start again' four times. The first two attempts, thoughts popped into my head about writing this chapter. The next one, I started thinking about an email that needed sending. The final unsuccessful time, I found I was thinking about what was for lunch. On the fifth occasion, I really focused on the cloud formations outside my window: the predominantly white sky with little crevices of powder blue opening out; the slow, languorous movement of the clouds along the sky. I focused on that for around a full minute.

As it finished, I noticed I was peripherally far more aware of sounds around me, and the feeling of the chair supporting me, and how I felt a bit tired. That's good. By so completely shifting the focus of my attention, I'd reconnected with my surroundings, and switched off from the computer, emails, texts and everything else.

Sometimes people feel the intense need to take a nap during or after 'switching off'. That's your body telling you how it really feels. Keep your eyes open though. You may not be napping but you are resting, and you'll feel suitably refreshed afterwards.

HINT

- Why clouds? One of the important things about this chapter is switching off from modern life and all the stresses and strains it entails. Remember what Dr Frank Lipman said about identifying with nature's rhythms and cycles?

  By picking something in nature – such as clouds – that increases the power of your switching off and reconnecting. But by all means choose trees, or grass, or anything else in nature if you think that would work better.

  If there's not a cloud in the sky where you are – lucky you. Focus instead on the blue of the sky, the texture of the colour, the brightness and clarity of the sky. As you know from Chapter 1, Instant Relaxation, blue is a great colour for relaxation, so this can help you even more.

The (almost) last word on the 'Switch off' technique goes to writer Charlie Brooker. In a *Guardian* article entitled, 'Google Instant is trying to kill me', he wrote:

My attention span was never great, but modern technology has halved it, and halved it again, and again and again, down to an atomic level, and now there's nothing discernible left.

For Charlie, and those like him, I'd say: try switching off.

Switch off – the extended version

Just like everything in this book, 'Switch off – the extended version' only takes a minute to set up. But unlike the previous technique, the extended version then benefits you for a whole day.

It's best to do it at the weekend, and you'll find out why.

During the week, many of us are guilty of sometimes counting the minutes until the end of the working day, without stopping to 'smell the roses', so to speak. Sometimes, we can end up doing this throughout much of our lives. When we're stuck in traffic we wish we could get to work. When we're at work we wish we could get home. When we're at home we wish it was the weekend. And so on. Life starts to pass us by. As Laurel and Hardy once said, 'I dreamt I was awake and woke up to find myself still sleeping.'

So, to be awake to everything around you, have a go at 'Switching off – the extended version'.

1 *Pick a day when you're not working.*

2 *Switch stuff off in the house. Phone, email, internet, computer, TV, radio, iPod and anything else.* (1 minute)

3 *Enjoy your day with anything that doesn't involve technology. Read, talk, sit, sunbathe, go for a walk, nap . . .*

4 *Resist the urge to switch the computer or TV on. Just enjoy life. Have a different day.*

Notice the effect it has on your mood.

5 *At the end of the day, write a list of five things you enjoyed about switching off for the whole day. This is important. Because you can't switch off like that all day every day, but you can learn from what happened on your 'switched-off day', and use what you have learnt to help you relax in future.* (1 minute)

If you want to be really extreme on your day off, switch off or hide all the clocks in your house as well and take your watch off. This is not for everybody, of course, but it is the logical extension.

Did you know that Leonardo da Vinci excelled not just as a painter, but also as a sculptor, architect, musician, scientist, mathematician, engineer, inventor, anatomist, geologist, cartographer, botanist and writer? Would he have had time to find the inspiration and creative genius for all that if he'd been checking Twitter on his iPhone every five minutes? As I said before, technology is great, but I believe we need to regulate the quantity and quality of information coming in.

So, what happened with Simon? Well, after he'd switched everything off, something odd started to happen. As I talked him through what to do, he kept falling asleep. Right there in front of me. Just the very act of starting to switch off and do something different was enough to completely and utterly change his state. I kept having to wake him up! That's how relaxing it can be to switch off from technology.

If you find that you start falling asleep when you do 'switch off', that's fine. It's certainly your body telling you that you'd like to take a nap. But unless you've got half-an-hour to spare – do it with your eyes open. It has the same effect on you. Sometimes it's not good to be caught napping at your desk. And if you really have to have a nap, set an alarm so you don't drift off for too long.

Eventually Simon came to see the benefit of switching off with his eyes open. He says he started to notice things he hadn't noticed in a while around his flat, such as the bookshelves, with some of his favourite books on, or the comfy beanbag, which he really likes sitting in, but doesn't because he's always sitting at the table hunched over his computer.

He says it helped him to relax, but also appreciate his day more. Simon now 'switches off' up to five times a day. And he's even taken up playing chess again. When he was a child, chess helped him to relax because he absorbed himself so completely in the moment. So now he does that again, as an adult.

TO-DO LIST – REMINDERS

▶▶ Our minds need downtime to cope with all the uptime. When we finally manage to turn those screens off, along with all the other technology that simultaneously helps and intrudes into our lives, we can properly allow our brain to relax.

▶▶ Switch everything off. Phone, email, internet, computer, TV, radio, iPod and anything else. (1 minute)

▶▶ Look out of the window, and focus on the clouds, their patterns, formations, colours and movement. Focus for a full minute on them. If at any point you notice that you're thinking about something else, you must start the full minute again. (1 minute)

▶▶ Simply notice how this makes you feel. (If you are unable to concentrate for the full minute, and you keep having to go back to the start, this may be frustrating but it is a good sign. It means your brain has become accustomed to focusing on multiple things at once, and will benefit even more from this change in perspective.)

▶▶ For the extended version of 'switch off', switch everything off in the house. Phone, email, internet, computer, TV, radio, iPod and anything else. (1 minute) Then enjoy your day with anything that doesn't involve technology. Read, talk, sit, sunbathe, go for a walk, nap, treat yourself . . .

CHAPTER SEVEN

Chill (Movies)

Sonia was desperately unhappy with the way she looked. Through my eyes, she looked an attractive lady in her mid-forties. Not through hers though. When I asked her what she disliked about her appearance, she said, 'Fat arms, fat legs, fat waist, fat everywhere'. Her perception of the way she looked obviously affected her whole outlook on life.

I felt like my work was cut out with Sonia.

As hard as it may seem to believe, after just one minute of one of the techniques in this chapter, she'd burst into tears of gratitude. Because of the way she'd been feeling only a minute previously, I had to ask her, 'Are you sure those are "happy tears"?' She nodded. She had experienced a revelation about how she looked, and how the world saw her.

By using the techniques in this chapter, you'll be able to change the way you see yourself and other people. This can

75

have a strong, quick impact on your ability to deal with the stresses in your life.

You're going to use the power of visualisation to make four movies: three in your head, and one real. Get ready to be a movie director, by using:

▸▸ Floating Cam

▸▸ Love Cam

▸▸ Bubble Cam

▸▸ Real Cam

As you're probably realising as you go through this book, you have an important way to influence the stress you feel. Your imagination.

For example, if you think unhappy thoughts, you become unhappy. If you think stressed thoughts, you become stressed. But yes, there is a flip side. If you think calm and relaxed thoughts, then more calm, relaxation, potential happiness and contentment can be yours.

This is not about denying your current state. I know how hard it is when life is difficult and you're worried, upset or stressed. I've been there myself. It's about gently and firmly leading yourself into a more positive state, step by step.

These techniques are especially good for a deep level of stress, because that is a level of worry and turbulence that becomes self-perpetuating.

Movie 1: Floating Cam

Let's focus on that link that people often talk about between body and mind. Can we really do something in a minute to benefit both? Yes. Floating Cam gets you to make physical changes to help your mental well-being. In addition, many find the sensation of floating enjoyable and peaceful.

1   *Sit down. Shut your eyes.*

2   *Imagine yourself floating up out of your seat, and over to a camera suspended in mid-air. You end up behind this floating camera, watching yourself right now.*

3   *As you look at yourself, notice any aspects of your physical appearance that don't look totally relaxed.*

4   *Float around and look at yourself from different angles. What could the person you are looking at physically do to relax further? Could they alter their posture, or seating position, or the position of their head, neck, arms, fingers, body, legs, feet and toes? Could they relax their facial muscles? Notice all this as you look at yourself through Floating Cam.*

5   *Now leave Floating Cam behind and float back to your seat.* (1 minute)

6   *Make all the little physical adjustments you need to make to feel more relaxed. (Although you may well find you've made the adjustments already.)*

Whenever you feel physically stressed, exhausted, tense or angry, you can switch on Floating Cam. And make the physical changes you need to start to relax.

HINT

■ All this visualisation can be a bit weird and wacky at first. When I started doing this, I would try to 'see myself', and I was trying so hard my brain was beginning to hurt. Sometimes, I just couldn't see what I was supposed to.

Eventually, I started to be able to tentatively 'see' things the way I wanted to. It takes a lot of getting used to, so keep at it.

My tip is that it often takes an initial 20/30 seconds to adjust to imagine looking at yourself through the lens of a movie camera, or even longer. That's fine. Be patient, until you've adjusted your perspective. It gets easier with practice. Now I use visualisation techniques like this every day.

Movie 2: Love Cam

Everyone wants to feel loved, right?

Love Cam makes use of the most important emotion of them all, and can have a startling impact. It works because sometimes it's important to remind ourselves of the positive and amazing way that other people think about us. When we remember this, it can alter the way we feel about ourselves.

1 *Imagine you are sitting opposite a movie camera.*

2 *Imagine floating out of your seat, and over to the video camera. Start to look at yourself through the video camera, still sitting there.*

3 *Now think of somebody who loves you. It may be a parent, husband, wife, son or daughter or friend. All that matters is that they love you for who you are.*

4 *Imagine that you are that person, looking through the video camera at you. Notice how they feel about you. What is it they love about you and appreciate about you? Fully appreciate and associate with that love. Notice how they love you the way you are. Do this for a full minute.*

5 *Float back into your body. And now feel that love you've experienced inside you. (1 minute)*

If you're feeling down, it can come as quite an intense experience to remember that you are accepted and loved as a good person. When you're anxious or stressed, or when you just want to feel good, switch on Love Cam.

Back to Sonia. When I asked her how she saw herself, she was agitated. 'Fat arms, fat legs, fat waist, fat everywhere.' When I told her about the Love Cam technique, you might have thought I'd asked her to bungee jump off the Eiffel Tower. She looked at me like I was crazy. But I explained how it worked, and she eventually decided to go for it.

I asked her to think about somebody who loved her. She picked her son. We started the technique and she imagined herself sitting there. Then she floated up and over, and looked at herself through the camera lens. She wrinkled her nose in disgust at what she saw.

Then she imagined she was her son, and looked through the camera at herself. As she looked, I reminded her to imagine exactly what her son would be thinking as he looked at his mother, with all the love and affection that he felt for her. The change was astonishing. Her face relaxed. She smiled. Then the tears started rolling down Sonia's face.

As she floated back into her body, she was still crying. I asked her if they were 'happy tears'. She nodded. She simply said that the moment she realised how her son looked at her, her worries about her appearance seemed much less important. That wasn't the end of the issue for her. But it was a key start in changing the way that she felt about herself. After that, she embarked on a daily regime of visualisation, as well as doing some of the techniques in Chapter 2, Quiet, to quieten that destructive 'inner voice'.

The world doesn't change in a minute. But it only takes a minute to start changing *your* world. That might sound cheesy, but it is true.

Movie 3: Bubble Cam

This technique is good for stressful situations, and for dealing with stressful people.

1 *Sit down and shut your eyes. Imagine watching a movie of you walking around your house. (Or somewhere you feel safe and secure.) Step right inside the movie now, and see everything exactly as you would see it.*

2 *Imagine being wrapped in a strong, protective, clear bubble. Put yourself right in the picture. Fill the bubble with all the positive energy you have. The bubble acts as a shield, protecting all your positive energy. Watch yourself as you walk around inside.*

3   *As you look around the bubble, think about a time when you felt really calm and strong. Make the colours, sounds and feelings vivid as you look around your bubble. Give the bubble your favourite colour so that when you look through Bubble Cam the world has a slight tint. (1 minute)*

4   *Now imagine going for a walk down your street. How good does it feel to be protected in Bubble Cam?*

5   *Nothing harmful can get in. Imagine something stressful (energy/words) flying towards you and splat! It hits the clear, protective bubble and just drips off. Ha! Unlucky! (1 minute)*

6   *Whenever you're in a stressful situation, switch on Bubble Cam. Your shield goes up. Notice how much stronger and more powerful, and safe you feel.*

One of the great things about Bubble Cam is that, with practice, it only takes a minute to switch on, but you can keep it on for as long as you like. Every time you switch it on though, remember to go through the full process of looking around your bubble and remembering that calm, strong time first.

Movie 4: Real Cam

All these movies going on in your head are one thing. Now let's make use of modern technology to create some real movies. All you need for this is anything that can take a video. A traditional camcorder or video camera, or just about any modern smartphone will do the job perfectly. Even most laptops can take videos now.

You've seen how visualising a 'good movie' can have an important effect on how you feel. Might the effect be even more powerful when you are watching a real movie?

1 *Decide on a place or situation that you feel relaxed in. It might be a family lunch, sitting at home, an afternoon picnic, hanging out with friends, a beautiful beach, field, mountain where you love to visit and walk, the view from a hotel on holiday.*

2 *Film it for one minute. Make sure to get it all in, and capture this moment at its very best. (1 minute)*

3 *Watch Real Cam when you feel stressed. Give it your full attention, and notice how you instantly start to feel more relaxed when you associate with this brilliant movie. (1 minute)*

HINT

■ I've got lots of Real Cam movies that I've shot and saved on my mobile phone. Here are two that work really well for me.

The first is the view from a desert town called Barreal on holiday in Argentina. The sky is blue, and as the camera pans around, way-off in the distance you can see the snow-capped Andes. I zoom in a little bit. You can see for miles, but there's not a road, house or person in sight. Just nature, desert and, in the distance, those far-off mountains. As I watch the video, I can hear the light rustle of the wind, and nothing else.

The second movie is just twenty seconds long, and I took it while at the Munich Oktoberfest. There I am, surrounded by friends, dancing on tables, goofing about, having fun on my friend Sam's stag do. We're all going bonkers. The happiness, the fun and the friendship makes me laugh every time I see it. It has a powerful, positive effect on me when I watch it.

I've found the more I do this, the more I actually enjoy the process of shooting the movie. This becomes visualisation of a different kind, as you start to work out in your head the best angles to shoot your Real Cam movie.

Whether you're like Sonia and use movies in your head, or like me at Oktoberfest using a real video, you can start to use visualisation as a powerful way to change the way you feel when you need it most.

TO-DO LIST – REMINDERS

▸▸ *Floating Cam:* Using visualisation, watch yourself from the perspective of a floating movie camera. What could the person you are looking at do physically to relax further? Make all the little adjustments necessary. By relaxing your body, your mind can start to relax too. (1 minute)

▸▸ *Love Cam:* Using visualisation, imagine floating over to a movie camera and looking at yourself through the eyes of a loved one. What is it they love and appreciate about you? Fully appreciate and associate with that love. (1 minute)

▸▸ *Bubble Cam:* Using visualisation, this is good for stressful situations. Imagine being surrounded by a strong, protective, clear bubble. Put yourself right in the picture. Fill the bubble with all the positive energy you have. Splat! Nothing bad can get in; it just drips down the side, while all that good energy protects you inside your bubble. (1 minute)

TO-DO LIST – REMINDERS *cont.*

▶▶ *Real Cam:* Decide on a place or situation that you feel relaxed in. Film it for one minute. Make sure to get it all in, and capture this moment at its very best. Then watch Real Cam when you feel stressed. (1 minute)

CHAPTER EIGHT

Chill (Music)

Jenny's daily journey to work took her over a long, high bridge in Scotland. She had to cross this bridge to get to work and back, and every morning Jenny would get seriously stressed and upset about driving over it. She said she knew it was illogical, but just like other people were scared of spiders, or flying, she would become extremely nervous when driving over bridges.

Every morning, she would break into a cold sweat as she thought about her forthcoming drive across the bridge. It wasn't so bad that it stopped her leaving the house, but it was an uncomfortable experience just getting to work. And then around lunchtime, she'd start thinking about the journey home, and that would stress her out all afternoon.

Jenny had started to even consider changing jobs, so she wouldn't have to drive across the bridge.

If you're somebody who gets stressed, tense or uptight, listening to music is a powerful way to change your mood. Listening to songs that remind you of good relaxing times works well, because your brain is reminded of the positive emotional state you felt, and fires it off again.

The idea of using music to relax dates back thousands of years. But of course these days, we have computers, iPods and ringtones, which mean we can use music to change the way we feel more effectively than ever.

This chapter suggests three ways to use music to relax:

▶▶ Your relax song

▶▶ Your relax ringtone

▶▶ Your relax playlist.

Have you ever heard a song on your iPod or radio that triggers old feelings from the past? The way music can relax us and help us to feel more positive is very significant. Of course, music can also make us feel sad, so we're going to carefully consider what you listen to when looking to change your state.

Your relax song

Lyrics, tone and rhythm can all have a big effect on your emotional state. If you want a demonstration of this, first listen to Bill Withers, 'Lovely Day'. Then listen to Daniel Powter, 'Bad Day'.

Bill Withers sample lyrics:

A lovely day - lovely day, lovely day, lovely day, lovely day.
Lovely day, lovely day, lovely day, lovely day.
A lovely day - lovely day, lovely day, lovely day, lovely day, etc.

Daniel Powter sample lyrics:

Had a bad day (Oh, had a bad day), Had a bad day,
  (Oh, yeah, yeah, yeeeeah)
Had a bad day (Oh, had a bad day), Had a bad day...
  Had a bad day...

How does listening to these two very different songs about a day affect your mood and thinking? It won't surprise you to hear that many people find listening to Bill Withers rather more uplifting than Daniel Powter singing about his miserable day. But not everyone. And that's the beautiful thing about music. Because we all have individual emotional associations with music that make us feel a certain way. For example, when Daniel Powter himself listens to 'Bad Day', he probably reflects on having written one of the most played songs on radio ever, and goes on to have a very good day.

So have a good think about all the songs on your iPod. Which one – more than any other – makes you feel really relaxed? For many people this will be something relatively calm and low tempo, but as discussed, it could be any song. Just so long as you're aware of the wonderfully relaxing and calming effect it has on you.

1 *Save it in an easy-to-find place on your computer/phone/ iPod/anywhere else where you listen to music. (1 minute)*

2 *Listen to a minute of the song now. As you listen, load even more emotional significance onto the song by thinking closely about a time when you felt really relaxed. See exactly what you saw, make the colours vivid and bright, and remember the feelings of well-being and relaxation you felt as you listen. (1 minute)*

3 *Listen to it whenever you need to quickly relax. (1 minute)*

Note: Sometimes the power of your relax song can diminish over time. It's just because we get used to it. So, after a while, switch it to something else relaxing. Remember to go through the same process of loading extra emotional significance onto it.

HINT

■ Having trouble working out what song to pick? It can sometimes be best to pick a song without lyrics. This is so you can control the messages your brain focuses on, rather than letting the lyrics influence them. ('Cos you had a bad day, had a bad day, had a bad day', etc.).

Recently I was asked to put together a list of self-help songs for iTunes. Here are three of the songs without lyrics that I picked. You can find the full list of songs on iTunes.

▸▸ *Sonata for two pianos in D Major, Mozart:* A lot of people say to me that listening to calming music before an exam really helps. Research seems to back this up. In one test, students who listened to this piece of Mozart performed significantly better than those who didn't.

HINT *cont.*

▶▶ *'Look Up', Zero 7:* Zero 7 in Manchester was definitely the most chilled gig I ever went to. I particularly like the title of this song – 'Look Up'. When we're feeling introspective and unhappy we often look down. Next time you are feeling down, look up high and see if it is easier to feel neutral, or more positive about things.

▶▶ *Japanese classical music:* Before an event some sports-men and women want to pump themselves up, but some want to calm themselves down. A famous heavyweight boxer apparently listens to Japanese classical music before he goes into the ring. I'm not a huge expert on Japanese classical music, but I just had a listen to some and it was rather soothing. Search for 'traditional Japanese music' if you're interested.

▶▶ *Your relax ringtone:* If you really want to start feeling more relaxed at a moment when you least expect it, set this song as your mobile phone ringtone. Then notice the effect it has on you when your phone rings. (1 minute to set up)

One of the ways this works so well is that the very nature of a phone means you start listening to your relax song when you least expect it. I've found this can be quite an odd and unexpectedly welcome interruption at surprising times. And you can get creative with this. The author Stephen Fry says in the foreword to the book, *Thanks Johnners*, by Jonathan Agnew, that he has a famously funny sporting commentary cock-up as a ringtone on his phone. He turns to it 'whenever he feels homesick or unhappy'. Why? Because presumably it helps him to feel happier, feel good and relax.

On many phones you can simply set your ringtone by picking a track from your collection. Alternatively, it costs almost nothing to buy ringtones on music websites.

Note: As with your relax song, it's worth changing your relax ringtone every once in a while. It's because we get used to hearing the same song, and so the power of the music can diminish. So, after a while, switch your ringtone to something else relaxing.

Your relax playlist

We can't necessarily flip instantly from 'stressed' to 'relaxed'. The relax playlist works on the theory that if you get really tight and tense and stressed, some people find it hard to instantly tell themselves to relax, and sometimes they just need a little bit longer.

It only takes a minute to set up your playlist, and you then have something you can listen to at any time, while doing other things. You can allow it to lead you slowly and effectively through the emotional states from stressed through neutral to relaxed.

It works by using a process called 'chaining anchors'. This means that you take your current emotional state, and slowly and carefully lead it by the hand into a more relaxed one. Think of it as like slowly ushering an elderly relative by the arm into their favourite comfy armchair so they can feel nice and relaxed.

Now grab your iPod and pick four songs:

1 *a song that you feel neutral about*

2 *a song that you find quite relaxing*

3 *a song that you find very relaxing – one of your favourites*

4 *your all-time most calming song (perhaps the song you've picked for your relaxation song earlier).*

Make a playlist on your iPod and put these four songs in it in the correct order. Call it 'My Relax Playlist'. If you don't have an mp3 player, make a CD, or even a good old-fashioned mix-tape. (1 minute)

Then listen whenever you want to feel more calm and be aware that one of the benefits of the relax playlist is that you can do anything else at the same time.

Important: Make sure you resist the temptation to load the playlist with four favourite songs. They must go from a song you feel neutral about through to a song that completely relaxes you. That is how you chain one emotional state to another.

Jenny's phobia of bridges happens to be a fairly common one, along with spiders, heights and flying. We approached her drive to work in three sections. First we ran the Rock Star Phobia Cure in Chapter 2, Calm, to make the deep background changes. Then she did the Bubble Cam visualisation from the previous chapter to make her feel safer. Then we looked at how she could use music. She decided to use the relax playlist rather than relax ringtone, as she only wanted to be more relaxed at a very specific time of the day.

One of the good things about setting up the playlist is that it's always enjoyable going through your music collection and picking out some favourite tunes. In itself, it is a relaxing way to spend some time. Once Jenny had made her choice, it took her just one minute to ready her playlist, and then she could simply press 'play' on her way to work.

As she drove towards the bridge, she pressed 'play', and allowed her playlist to do its work. She found it made a huge difference to her journey and she felt far more neutral and 'normal' when driving across the bridge itself.

By the way, after a couple of months, Jenny noticed that her relax playlist wasn't working so well. She'd just got used to the songs (and a bit bored of them), so she picked some new ones and the playlist started to work effectively again.

TO-DO LIST – REMINDERS

▶▶ *Your relax song:* Have a good think about all the songs you own. Which one – more than any other – makes you feel really calm? Load even more feelings of relaxation onto it, by listening to it and remembering a time when you felt utterly relaxed. (1 minute)

Then listen to it whenever you want to instantly feel that way. (1 minute)

▶▶ *Your relax ringtone:* If you really want to start feeling more relaxed at times when you least expect it – set this song as your mobile phone ringtone. Then notice the effect it has on you when your phone rings. (1 minute)

▶▶ *Your relax playlist:* If you find it really hard to de-stress and unwind, set up a playlist with four songs – from a song you feel neutral about, to a song that absolutely makes you feel calm and chilled out. (1 minute)

Simply press play before you want to start feeling more relaxed, and get on with whatever you were doing while you listen.

CHAPTER NINE

The Postcard Plan

Dave enjoyed his job in the music business, but it was incredibly busy. He would say that he had to 'go into work mode' just to get everything done. Things were just a 'work mode' blur between 8 a.m. and 5 p.m. By 5 p.m., things were starting to calm down, and the last couple of hours of the day were always the most productive. He'd leave work about 7 p.m. He would have loved to be able to leave earlier but he had too much work to do. Besides, most of the others in the office stayed until 7 p.m. anyway, so it might have been a bit frowned upon to go home early.

Dave normally got home about 8 p.m., which often meant that he had only half-an-hour with the kids before they went to bed. In fact, he had only a couple of hours at home before he himself went to bed, ready to get up again at 6 a.m.

Dave had tried to make changes to reduce his workload on quite a few occasions so he could get home earlier to spend more time with his kids. But every time he did this, after a few weeks he'd let it slip and revert back to the old, hectic working day. He knew he should sort it out once and for all, but he just couldn't help himself.

His kids helped him to relax from his busy job more than anything. And yet he didn't spend enough time with them.

This chapter is about making a commitment to change permanently as well as instantly. And it still only takes a minute.

We are now getting towards the end of the book and hopefully you've found the instant techniques that work well for you. I'm sure some worked better than others, and that's fine – after all, we're all different.

I have already said how important it is to write stuff down – about the proven link between the act of writing and the brain committing to a goal. I can hardly get anything done without writing it down. If you were to take a walk around my kitchen right now you'd see all kinds of signs, written notes and pinned-up reminders on the fridge – buying a pint of milk, my exact schedule for the day, how many times I'll check my email, etc.

This chapter combines the effectiveness of writing something down with the power of a public commitment.

Commitment

Commitment is acknowledged in many studies as one of the most powerful tools in achieving goals. We like to think of ourselves as consistent. And we especially like other people to think about us as consistent. So, if we tell other people about our goal, we are more likely to stick to it.

Did you know that many donations are achieved this way? First we are asked to sign a petition for a cause, or join up online. Then we're asked for a donation. Because it is consistent with our public commitment of signing up, we're more likely to give. And it's not out of obligation either; we *want* to give even more too.

Have a look at the 'Postcard Plan'. It works like this:

▶▶ *Thinking about your goal is the first stage of doing it.*

▶▶ *By deciding on it, that's the first level of commitment.*

▶▶ *By writing it down, that's the next level of commitment.*

▶▶ *By posting it to yourself, you take it to a whole new level of commitment: dating it, postmarking it and committing it to posterity.*

▶▶ *And finally, by doing what everybody does with postcards, sticking it up on the fridge so everybody can see it – that's the final level of commitment.*

In the area of relaxation, I've found this commitment to be vital. Because many of us know we should be doing more to look after ourselves in this area, but we sometimes just kind of let it slip. Other things get in the way.

Well, not any more. Let's make a commitment to you feeling more relaxed, long term.

Things are changing around here

Decide on one daily thing you will change, permanently. It should be something that will make a significant difference to your life. It may be a technique that you've read in this book, or it may be a specific personal change that you can make to your day or lifestyle. Make sure it's something achievable.

Examples

▶▶ *Going for a long walk every morning, and doing 'The Float' technique (Chapter 1, Instant Relaxation) at the same time.*

▶▶ *Listening to your relaxation playlist (Chapter 8, Chill (Music)) every day on the way to work.*

▶▶ *Finishing work an hour earlier.*

▶▶ *Switching the computer off at 6 p.m. and not checking your emails again until the next morning.*

▶▶ *Reading a book in the evening instead of watching TV.*

▶▶ *'Bouncing' or using 'The Spot', or using a relaxation playlist, daily visualisation, or any of the many other techniques in this book.*

When you've made your mind up, make sure it's *possible* to take this action. Make sure you're *able* to do it. And, most importantly, make sure you *want* to do it. (Because, if you don't, it's not going to last very long!)

And then, check that making this change won't negatively affect any other area of your life.

For instance, Dave knew he was spending too long at work, but he wasn't being strict with himself about getting home in time to see the kids before they went to bed.

In the bigger scheme of things, he knew that hanging out with his children was more important than finishing work an hour later. Was there a way that Dave could get his work done, *and* get back to see the kids before bedtime? Was there a way he could commit to this goal, and then stick to it?

The Postcard Plan in practice

1 *Now that you have your relax goal, get a postcard and write it down. (You can log on to www.tonywrighton.com and get your Postcard Plan template.) (1 minute)*

2 *Date the postcard with the exact future date by which you'd like to have achieved your relaxation goal.*

3 *Address it to yourself and post it. Post it second-class so it takes a few extra days, and arrives as a nice reminder and a bit of a surprise.*

4 *Pin it up on the fridge or somewhere where you and everyone else in the house can see it. Your name. Your address. Your commitment to being relaxed. Stamped, postmarked and dated for posterity.*

HINT

■ It may sound obvious – but pin the postcard up so the written side is visible. My friend Jim thought the Postcard Plan was a great idea. A few weeks later I went round to his house and he proudly showed me his fridge – with a lovely postcard of the sights of London displayed! What he'd written to himself was completely invisible to him and his family as it was face down.

When you discover how well it works, you might even want to send yourself a few different Postcard Plans. Of course the principles behind the postcard work with anything that you've decided, written down, told people about and pinned up somewhere.

Important: When you have a little lapse, or hit a challenge, go back to the Postcard Plan, and have a look at it, and remember why it's important to you. I say that because none of us always does everything exactly as we intend to. The important thing is to remember that when you hit a challenge – you forget to do your relaxation routine in the morning, or you forget to give yourself some quiet time in the middle of the day – to realise that just by noticing you've not done it, that's a good thing, and can make you more likely to do it next time.

Before Dave sent himself a postcard he ran through the ramifications of permanently leaving work slightly earlier. He decided to talk to his boss, who gave it the green light. So he knew it was *possible*, he knew he was *able* to do it and he definitely *wanted* to do it.

The reason the Postcard Plan worked so well with Dave is that the rest of his family could see the postcard he'd sent himself stuck on his fridge. His commitment was public, for all his family to see. When he lapsed a couple of times and stayed late at work, his kids cheekily pointed out his Postcard Plan on the fridge, which said he'd be home from work by 6.30 p.m. Signed 'Dad'. Dated, and displayed for everyone to see.

Of course, there was the odd occasion when Dave did have to stay late for work. But after he sent himself the Postcard Plan, it was just that. The odd occasion. And sometimes, if Dave did have to work in the evening, he started to bring the work home. At least that way he'd still get to see the children, who always had a positive influence on his mood, even if he had to knuckle down and finish things off once they went to bed.

TO-DO LIST – REMINDERS

▶▶ Decide on one daily thing you will change, permanently, in your quest for relaxation. It should be something that will make a significant difference to your life. It may well be a technique that you've read in this book, or it may be a specific personal change that you can make to your day or lifestyle.

▶▶ Get a postcard and write your relax goal on it. Above it, write the date by which you'd like to have achieved it.
(1 minute)

TO-DO LIST – REMINDERS *cont.*

▶▶ **Send yourself your postcard. When it arrives back, pin it on the fridge.** (1 minute)

▶▶ **Your commitment to being more relaxed long term is there for everybody to see. You've thought about it, written it down, put your own name and address on it, dated it, postmarked it and then displayed it.**

CHAPTER TEN

The Future

Remember Jenny from Chapter 8, Chill (Music)? Her daily journey to work took her over a long, high bridge in Scotland. And this wasn't ideal as she had a phobia of bridges, and of being on them.

Every morning, she would break into a cold sweat as she thought about her forthcoming drive across the bridge. But by using some of the techniques in this book – Rock Star Phobia Cure, Bubble Cam and setting up a relax playlist – she began to feel less anxious about her journey to work. As she admitted, she wouldn't say that she necessarily enjoyed it, but she felt far more relaxed when driving across the bridge itself than she had in the past.

Fast forward a few years and Jenny is now working at a different job that doesn't involve driving across a bridge twice a day. She very rarely drives across bridges now. Perhaps because of this, she told me how she was in the car one day and noticed a creeping anxiety when

she approached a bridge. She felt like she had forgotten some of the techniques that worked so well in helping her to relax.

There are two very good reasons for this final chapter.

The first is that people have short memories, so we're going to make a written record of what works well for you.

The second is that there is something else you can use in the future to become *really good* at relaxation, which I haven't mentioned yet. And that is by learning from other people, by finding out how successful, happy, well-rounded people do it, from American presidents, to famous drummers, to your next-door neighbour, to anyone who might be able to help you take your relaxation skills to the next level.

As you know, all the techniques in this book take one minute. But we mustn't just focus on the 'now'. I want you to be more relaxed long term as well as instantly. What would be the point in going to all the effort of buying this book, practising the techniques, making the changes, and then six months or a year down the line forgetting what it was that worked so well? You'd have to do all that hard work all over again.

You've already had a chance to plan longer term with the Postcard Plan in Chapter 9. Now, this chapter, 'The Future', will end up being your relaxation diary.

The diary

George Washington was the first US president, and acclaimed 'father of his country'. And he loved writing diaries. He wrote diaries on politics, diaries on war, diaries on travel, diaries on specific events, diaries on farming conditions and even diaries on the weather. These diaries were very important to him. Once he went on a long trip to Philadelphia and forgot his diary. He sent an order to forward it on immediately. 'It will be found, I presume, on my writing table,' he said. 'Put it under a good strong paper cover, sealed up as a letter.'

Why did he write so much down? He realised the importance of being a visionary, planning for the future, but also of recording what he did with his time and returning to consult those notes at important times. He said:

We should not look back unless it is to derive useful lessons from past errors, and for the purpose of profiting by dearly bought experience.

The most effective way to be really good at relaxing and changing your state is working out exactly what works really well for you: writing it down; and then coming back and reading it again when you need a reminder of how to access deep feelings of relaxation and calm. Just like Washington, you can then profit from your 'dearly bought experience', and indeed 'derive useful lessons from past errors'.

You need reminders. We all do. I can't remember what I had for dinner last night; let alone what I did six months ago. So to really plan for the future, write down what worked so well. And it still only takes a minute.

There is another reason for this. I've deliberately designed different relaxation techniques that will work better for different people. For example, if you're someone who responds very well to visual stuff, Chill (Movies) might help you see things more clearly. Or if you're someone who is more auditory, then Chill (Music) might sound more relaxing. Everyone's different, so work out what bits you like, and then write them down. It is the same process that I used for the final chapter in my book *Confidence in a Minute* and many people have said it's the final piece in the jigsaw for permanent change.

You write down:

▶▶ *the occasion*

▶▶ *what you did and how it worked*

▶▶ *your relaxation rating (marks out of ten). Often we forget how well something has worked. This will help you remember.*
(1 minute)

Perhaps it was a technique you used, a relaxation method, a movie you watched in your mind, music you listened to or something else.

When you do this, you'll have a guide on how to relax *written in your own words* when you next pick up this book. It'll be your personal guide.

OCCASION: A best-man speech at a wedding.

WHAT I DID AND HOW IT WORKED: The Spot (Chapter 1). Even just thinking about a time I felt more relaxed helped me to feel more comfortable on the big day. Then, in the moment before my speech, I looked at my blue spot. I instantly remembered a time when I made a small, confident speech to some work colleagues. It helped me to relax.

RELAX RATING OUT OF TEN: 8

OCCASION: Couldn't get to sleep last night.

WHAT I DID AND HOW IT WORKED: I used the Breathing by Numbers technique (Chapter 3). It helped calm me down but didn't actually help me to drop off. Tomorrow I'll try the Getting to Sleep technique (Chapter 4) instead.

RELAX RATING OUT OF TEN: 4

OCCASION: Feeling generally anxious about going back to work.

WHAT I DID AND HOW IT WORKED: Used Floating Cam (Chapter 8) to calm myself down. I especially noticed the tension in my face. When I relaxed all the little muscles around my forehead, I could feel myself physically relaxing. That helped me start to feel calmer.

RELAX RATING OUT OF TEN: 6

OCCASION:

WHAT I DID AND HOW IT WORKED:

RELAX RATING OUT OF TEN:

OCCASION:

WHAT I DID AND HOW IT WORKED:

RELAX RATING OUT OF TEN:

OCCASION:

WHAT I DID AND HOW IT WORKED:

RELAX RATING OUT OF TEN:

OCCASION:

WHAT I DID AND HOW IT WORKED:

RELAX RATING OUT OF TEN:

OCCASION:

WHAT I DID AND HOW IT WORKED:

RELAX RATING OUT OF TEN:

OCCASION:

WHAT I DID AND HOW IT WORKED:

RELAX RATING OUT OF TEN:

OCCASION:

WHAT I DID AND HOW IT WORKED:

RELAX RATING OUT OF TEN:

OCCASION:

WHAT I DID AND HOW IT WORKED:

RELAX RATING OUT OF TEN:

OCCASION:

WHAT I DID AND HOW IT WORKED:

RELAX RATING OUT OF TEN:

OCCASION:

WHAT I DID AND HOW IT WORKED:

RELAX RATING OUT OF TEN:

Consult this part of the book whenever you want to feel more relaxed in future.

Learning from others

The drummer Charlie Watts rose to worldwide fame with one of the world's most successful bands – the Rolling Stones. The band has had 92 singles, 29 studio albums, 10 live albums (and counting), has been inducted into the Rock and Roll Hall of Fame, and he himself has been inducted into the Modern Drummer Hall of Fame. So how on earth did he learn to play the drums?

When I was a kid I never learned to play. I actually got in bands through watching people play and copying them.

That's right. Charlie Watts never actually took lessons in how to play the drums. He watched other people do it. And then copied them.

Now what could you do by watching other people? It would seem that this is intuitive to us because we've been doing this for as long as we can remember. According to behavioural psychology, the way babies learn to speak is by copying their parents (and everyone else with whom they come into contact). There is a growing body of research on the ability of adult human beings to learn by imitation. If you want to give a name to this technique, it's 'modelling'.

When it comes to relaxation, find other people who are good at it, and do what they do. Who do you know who is really good at relaxing? What do they do? How do they do it? Where do they do it? When? Why? What do they believe is important about being relaxed?

So when somebody does something relaxing well, make a note of:

▶▶ *who you studied*

▶▶ *what worked for them*

▶▶ *what happened when you did it*

▶▶ *a relax rating out of ten.*

By the way, you might learn from people you know, or you might learn from people in the public eye. For example, you could look at a sportsman's pre-match routine, or a performer's breathing exercises before they go on stage, or even someone like the Dalai Lama. The possibilities are endless when you think about how you can get better at relaxing.

PERSON STUDIED: Caroline in the office.

WHAT WORKS FOR THEM: Says she works out every morning before work because it helps her to relax and clear her mind.

WHAT WORKS FOR ME: The physical exercise really helped me to feel good. The harder I work out, the more I seemed to clear my head.

RELAX RATING OUT OF TEN: 9

PERSON STUDIED: A famous footballer.

WHAT WORKS FOR THEM: Before a game, he sits in a dark room and shuts his eyes and focuses on what's ahead.

WHAT WORKS FOR ME: Not a great deal. I found I was too tense and excited with nervous energy to sit still for too long.

RELAX RATING OUT OF TEN: 4

PERSON STUDIED: Jen, my friend.

WHAT WORKS FOR THEM: She only listens to classical music in the car. She says it gives her crucial 'me time' to think, reflect, and relax before and after the stresses of the working day.

WHAT WORKS FOR ME: Wow – I felt so chilled out when I arrived at work. I found I was able to relax but also think about the day ahead. It didn't work quite so well on the way home because of a traffic jam – stressful! But I will do it again as it felt good.

RELAX RATING OUT OF TEN: 8

PERSON STUDIED:
WHAT WORKS FOR THEM:

WHAT WORKS FOR ME:

RELAX RATING OUT OF TEN:

PERSON STUDIED:
WHAT WORKS FOR THEM:

WHAT WORKS FOR ME:

RELAX RATING OUT OF TEN:

PERSON STUDIED:
WHAT WORKS FOR THEM:

WHAT WORKS FOR ME:

RELAX RATING OUT OF TEN:

PERSON STUDIED:
WHAT WORKS FOR THEM:

WHAT WORKS FOR ME:

RELAX RATING OUT OF TEN:

PERSON STUDIED:
WHAT WORKS FOR THEM:

WHAT WORKS FOR ME:

RELAX RATING OUT OF TEN:

PERSON STUDIED:
WHAT WORKS FOR THEM:

WHAT WORKS FOR ME:

RELAX RATING OUT OF TEN:

PERSON STUDIED:
WHAT WORKS FOR THEM:

WHAT WORKS FOR ME:

RELAX RATING OUT OF TEN:

Now you've got your own personal journal of what works best for you, and other people too.

Jenny had made some positive changes after we first met. Her fear of bridges and driving over them was serious, but she had discovered a range of useful ways that she could help herself to relax before going on her journey to work. Three years later, she's working somewhere different, and notices that 'creeping anxiety' as she approaches a high bridge in Scotland.

So she went home and dug out the 'relaxation diary' I had asked her to keep at the time. In it, she'd written all the techniques she's used, and even handily given them marks out of ten. There was the Rock Star Phobia Cure (she gave that 9/10). She ran the exercise through again and then carried on flicking through the pages. She found the 'Turn it Down' internal voice technique. She only gave that 2/10, so she knew not to use that one again. Ah! This one worked – the relax playlist. She gave that 7/10 at the time. That must have worked pretty well. So she set herself up a new playlist, and felt more relaxed again when she listened to it.

Because once you've felt a certain way in the past, you can feel that way whenever you like. Such as now…

DO WHAT WORKS – REMINDERS

▶▶ The most effective way to be really good at relaxing and changing your state is working out exactly what works well for you. Write it down. And then come back and read it again when you need a reminder on how to access deep feelings of relaxation and calm.

▶▶ Write down: the occasion, what technique you did, and how well it worked out of ten. (1 minute)

▶▶ Study other people who are great at relaxing and staying calm in stressful situations. Write down: what they do, what works for them, what works for you, and again, a mark out of ten. (1 minute)

▶▶ Whenever you want to feel more relaxed in the future, consult this chapter. It will end up being the most important chapter in the whole book, because it is a personal journal of what works best for you. (1 minute)

End bit

That's it. Thanks for reading. Are you feeling a bit more relaxed now? Hopefully you're now realising how you can start to make small changes in seconds. And of course, small changes lead to big ones.

If you've got this far and you haven't done everything in the book, go back with a spirit of curiosity and do the other exercises. Put a blue coloured spot on your wallet, alter your ringtone, start seeing yourself through the eyes of somebody who loves you, switch Facebook off and pick up a real book, start 'floating' and 'bouncing', send yourself a postcard, give yourself a 'virtual massage', and stare less into screens and more into the eyes of people.

And then, in the future, do what works best for you.

Acknowledgements

A huge thank you to Clare Wallis at Virgin Books for all her hard work and support on this book, I really appreciate it and it has been a hugely enjoyable process. Also enormous thanks go to Louisa Joyner and Davina Russell at Virgin who have been absent in the happiest of circumstances.

Thanks to James Wills, at Watson Little for his tenacity and enthusiasm. Thanks to Andy Hipkiss, who is the greatest agent, and supportive and well connected to boot.

Thanks to Matt Bowen from Matthew Bowen Media for the audiobook photos, and a big thank you to John Hirst of Create Media for offering numerous creative ideas as well as being such a good pal through the whole writing process.

Thank you to Doctor Steve, Kay Cooke and Lloydie for reading through, testing stuff out and offering their advice and encouragement. Thanks to my sister Louise for diverting attention away from her own wonderful book to looking over the drafts of this and being so supportive. Finally, thanks to Mum, for everything.

Index